Getting Through It Together

**A FAMILY GUIDE
to
THE COLLEGE APPLICATIONS PROCESS**

Susan McGarr, Ph.D.

outskirts press

Getting Through It Together
A Family Guide To The College Applications Process
All Rights Reserved.
Copyright © 2019 Susan McGarr, Ph.D.
V3.0 R1.2

The opinions expressed in this manuscript are solely the opinions of the author and do not represent the opinions or thoughts of the publisher. The author has represented and warranted full ownership and/or legal right to publish all the materials in this book.

This book may not be reproduced, transmitted, or stored in whole or in part by any means, including graphic, electronic, or mechanical without the express written consent of the publisher except in the case of brief quotations embodied in critical articles and reviews.

Outskirts Press, Inc.
http://www.outskirtspress.com

ISBN: 978-1-9772-1540-6

Cover Photo © 2019 www.gettyimages.com. All rights reserved - used with permission.

Outskirts Press and the "OP" logo are trademarks belonging to Outskirts Press, Inc.

PRINTED IN THE UNITED STATES OF AMERICA

To Tim and Lucy

Your love and laughter got me through this.

Thank you.

CONTENTS

INTRODUCTION		i
Chapter 1:	**PREPARING FOR THE COLLEGE APPLICATIONS PROCESS**	1
1.1	The College Application Timeline	2
	9th Grade - Freshman	2
	10th Grade - Sophomore	4
	11th Grade - Junior	7
	12th Grade - Senior	9
1.2	To Do list for Juniors and Seniors	11
1.3	Get to Know Yourself	14
1.4	Take Control	15
1.5	Study Tips	17
1.6	Notes for Students with Learning Differences	18
	1.6.1 Learning Differences at College	20
1.7	*Parent Pointer – Helping Your Teen on the College*	23
Chapter 2:	**ACADEMIC PREPARATION**	26
2.1	Academic Profile and Plan	27
	2.1.1 Grade Point Average (GPA)	29
	2.1.2 High Schools Classes Required for College	30
	2.1.3 Advanced Classes in High School	31
2.2.	Standardized Tests	33
	2.2.1 The SAT	33
	2.2.2 The ACT	34
	2.2.3 Scoring the SAT and ACT	34
	2.2.4 Super Scoring	37
	2.2.5 When to Take the Tests	38
	2.2.6 The SAT Subject Tests	39
	2.2.7 Test Optional	41
2.3	Preparing a Résumé	42
2.4	Letters of Recommendation	49
2.5	*Parent Pointer – How to Help in the Academic Stage*	51
Chapter 3:	**CHOOSING COLLEGES**	52
3.1	Getting Started on the College List	53
3.2	Considerations for Choosing Colleges	57
3.3	Types of Educational Institutions	61
3.4	Majors, Minors, and 'Areas of Interest'	62
3.5	ROTC (Reserve Officers' Training Corps)	64
3.6	College Search Resources	64
3.7	College Visits	72
3.8	College Interviews	77
3.9	Building your College Blueprint	82
3.10	*Parent Pointer – Help with Choosing Colleges*	87

Chapter 4:	**COLLEGE APPLICATIONS**	**91**
4.1	Types of Applications	92
4.2	Completing the Common Application	93
	4.2.1 Generic information	93
	4.2.2 Presenting Activities	93
	4.2.3 College Application Tips	95
4.3	Evaluation of Applications	96
	4.3.1 The Family Educational Rights and Privacy Act	100
4.4	Financial Aid	101
4.5	*Parent Pointer – Managing Expectations*	104
Chapter 5:	**COLLEGE APPLICATION WRITING:**	
	ESSAYS, PERSONAL STATEMENTS, AND SUPPLEMENTS	**105**
5.1	College Applications Essays	106
5.2	The Writing Process – The Basics	108
5.3	The Common Application Essay	110
	5.3.1 Guidelines on the Common Application Essay	111
5.4	Main Essays on Other Applications	118
	5.4.1 The Coalition Application Essay	118
	5.4.2 The Universal Application Essay	118
	5.4.3 The University of California Personal Insight Essays	119
5.5	Choosing a Style for your Essay	121
	5.5.1 The Narrative Essay	121
	5.5.2 The Personal Statement	124
5.6	The Dos and Don'ts of College Essay Writing	126
5.7	College-Specific Supplements	128
5.8	Writing for Scholarships, Honors, and Special Programs	132
5.9	The College Applications Essays and Supplements Tracker	135
5.10	*Parent Pointer – How to Help in the Essay-Writing Stage*	136
Chapter 6:	**SUBMISSIONS AND BEYOND**	**139**
6.1	College Admissions Plans	140
6.2	Submissions Schedule and Response Tracker	141
6.3	Responses: Acceptances, Deferrals, and Wait List	142
6.4	*Parent Pointer – Helping in the Decision-Making Process*	145
Chapter 7:	**ADVICE FOR INTERNATIONAL STUDENTS**	**146**
7.1	Studying in the United States	147
7.2	Admissions	148
7.3	Funding	149
7.4	Visas	150
7.5	Application Tips for International Students	151
A Final Word		**157**
Glossary		**158**
Resources		**166**
About the Author		**169**

INTRODUCTION

In the increasingly competitive landscape of college admissions, high school students can be more fearful than previous generations about their chances of getting into college. To be competitive, students enroll in challenging classes and take difficult tests. They also play sports, take on volunteer work, and participate in all sorts of activities, internships, and summer programs. Some manage to have a job too. Thinking about applying to college can be a daunting prospect to these busy students.

The college applications process is an enormous task. It takes energy, stamina, and patience to understand all that needs to be done and then to actually do it! The sheer volume of work involved in the planning and organizing of a student's life in preparation for college can be overwhelming for students and their families.

There is no simple way to manage all the facets of the college applications process, but it can be organized in such a way as to make it more accessible, manageable, and productive. That's what this book is about: In a no-frills way, it outlines what must be done, when, and how.
It helps students and their families navigate the various aspects of the process by providing:

- Information on tactical planning and preparation in high school;
- Details of the college application process;
- Tools to help you get organized and in control;
- Notes on how to build a college list to match aspirations and abilities;
- Guidance on how to prepare an outstanding college application;
- Advice on how to write compelling essays, personal statements, and supplements;
- Advice for international students who want to apply to college in the United States;
- Advice to parents on how to help their teen throughout the process; and
- Tips on how college admissions officers evaluate the applications.

The book is for students and parents specifically, but will be useful for anyone interested in helping a young person with their college applications process. It is deliberately forthright and, where relevant, information is condensed into lists and templates for ease of reading and reference.

This book is written in thanks to all the students and families with whom I have had the great privilege to work.

Susan McGarr, Ph.D.
Cirencester, 2019

CHAPTER 1

PREPARING FOR THE COLLEGE APPLICATIONS PROCESS

Life is either a daring adventure, or nothing at all.

- Helen Keller

1.1. THE COLLEGE APPLICATION TIMELINE

Preparing for college starts in high school. Below are details of those things you can be doing grade-by-grade. You will see some things repeated, such as, 'keep up your grades', whilst there are other things that should be done within a particular timeframe. Every item on the lists is explained in detail in the book and, where applicable, there are related organizational templates, questionnaires, or charts.

9TH GRADE – HIGH SCHOOL FRESHMAN

Your freshman year of high school is an important year in the college application process. The grades from your 9th grade are, in a sense, the foundation of your application: an indicator to college admissions officers of early academic interest and aptitude. Grades from 9th grade can be even more important when students with similar grades and test scores are being evaluated alongside each other. The student who demonstrates from the beginning of high school a high level of academic interest through good class choices and consistent high grades, will be an attractive candidate for colleges that look for students with academic promise, enthusiasm for learning, and commitment to excellence.

There are many things you can do to lay the groundwork for your high school years, all of which are listed below, but keep in mind these three most important tasks:

1) Take challenging classes;
2) Keep your grades up;
3) Participate in activities outside of the classroom.

UNDERSTAND THE COLLEGE APPLICATION PROCESS
Take time out to learn what to expect from the college application process. Knowing what you're doing and making a plan of action will ease the potential anxiety and fear that many students have around the process.

THINK ABOUT WHAT THE COLLEGE ADMISSIONS OFFICERS ARE LOOKING FOR IN APPLICANTS
It's easy to get caught up worrying about what YOU want in a college that you forget to think about what it is that college admissions officers are actually looking for in their applicants. As you start to build a picture of the types of colleges you might be interested in, make a note of the evaluation criteria and think about what you are doing to meet or exceed those expectations.

GET TO KNOW YOUR HIGH SCHOOL COUNSELOR AND/OR COLLEGE COUNSELOR
Your high school counselor is a very important person in your world: they are instrumental in many aspects of your high school experience and in preparation for college. It's a good idea to meet with your counselor early on to discuss your plan to go to college and the class options to help you achieve your goals. Your counselor can also give you information about colleges to which previous students have been admitted/attended.

TAKE CHALLENGING COURSES
No matter what you hear to the contrary, your academic record is the most important part of your college application. College admissions officers are not only looking for good grades, they are also looking for evidence that you have pushed yourself and taken the most challenging courses offered at your school. Research all the options for accelerated, honors, and Advanced Placement (AP) classes and enroll in those that you will give you the opportunity to shine.

PREPARING FOR THE COLLEGE APPLICATIONS PROCESS

KEEP UP YOUR GRADES
Grades are very important. And freshman grades matter as much as the sophomore and junior grades that will appear on your college application. Low grades in freshman year can particularly affect your chances of getting into selective colleges. When evaluated against applicants with similar grades, test scores, and GPA, the student with a record of consistent high grades will triumph over the 'shaky start' applicant.

READ BEYOND THE CLASSROOM
It cannot be stressed enough: reading makes you a better reader, writer, and critical thinker. It actually doesn't matter WHAT you read; it's just important to read beyond the required reading of your English class. Find books on subjects you enjoy. Like Science fiction films? Try reading the books first – believe me, they are always better!

SPORTS
Participating in sports demonstrates to admissions officers that you possess something that is rarely discussed, but often appreciated: discipline. It takes discipline – both physical and mental - to participate in an activity that requires commitment, dedication, and stamina. While you may not need to make a decision about whether or not to continue with a sport in which you have participated since you were three years old, it is certainly worthwhile thinking about what the sport means to you. Things to consider are:

1) Will I continue to play in college?
2) Am I good enough to continue playing in college?
3) Do I have enough TIME to play and practice and keep up my grades?

It might be helpful to write down your thoughts and look those over again next year.

EXTRACURRICULAR ACTIVITIES
If you have interests beyond the classroom, now is the time to focus on the one or two that you love. College admissions officers are not looking for QUANTITY when considering extracurricular activities; they are looking for commitment, passion, and engagement with one or two. If you are doing a sport, you already know that you don't have a lot of spare time. However, it is advisable to think about extending yourself and finding a volunteer activity or job that will 'round out' your profile and enhance your application. It should be noted that longevity accounts for a great deal more than variety, so a babysitting job that you've had since 9th grade and continued through to 11th grade (when applications are submitted) is a notable accomplishment for an extracurricular activity compared to one that you did for a few weeks in your rising senior summer with the obvious intention of getting something to 'put on the résumé.'

CONTINUE WITH A FOREIGN LANGUAGE
With increased globalization, the ability to communicate in more than one language is a valuable asset and one that colleges recognize as being another academic factor on which to evaluate a candidate for admission. Two to three years of foreign language in high school is generally required, but for a boost in your chances of admission to the more selective colleges, four years of foreign language will make you a more attractive candidate.

ASK FOR HELP IF YOU NEED IT
Don't waste a second in asking for help if you find yourself struggling in any subject. Once you get behind, it can be very difficult to turn yourself around at a later stage. Talking to your teacher and/or counselor,

arranging a study group with friends, or going to peer-tutored homework groups can all be an enormous help.

SAT II SUBJECT TESTS
Consider taking the SAT Subject test if:

- You have taken a year-long class in a subject in which there is a SAT subject test;
- You have done well in the class;
- It is a class that is only offered in 9th grade with no opportunity to continue study within high school.

For example, if you take World History in 9th grade and do well in the class, consider taking the SAT Subject test immediately at the end of that year. The ideal time to take the test is at the end of the school year, during or after finals, when the subject is still fresh in your mind, in May or June. If you do not do well on the test, you are not obliged to submit the score on a college application.

VISIT COLLEGES
As a 9th grader, you don't need to do serious college research trips, but if you happen to live near a college or are visiting an area with a college or colleges, it is worthwhile taking a walk around a few campuses to get a 'feel' for them and pay attention to the things you like and possibly dislike about each one. A College Visit/Research sheet is included in Chapter 3 and is a good place to start thinking about what may or may not be important to you.

FINANCES
College is a privilege and investment and you need to know what finances are involved and to what extent, if any, you have help with those costs. This is the time to sit down with your parents to discuss what contribution, if any, they are able to make towards your college education. Once you have a picture of that, you can then start to explore financing options and scholarships.

SUMMER EXPERIENCES
Although it is tempting to tell yourself that you need to chill out and relax over the summer, it is unwise to not use this valuable time for some form of self-improvement. A college course, a job, or a volunteer position as a little league coach all provide invaluable experience and material for your résumé and college application. Another option is to take a summer camp at a local college. It will give you the experience of a college-like atmosphere and, if you take a course to complement your interests, it will enhance your college application.

THINK AND VISUALIZE
Think about what you want. This is not as easy as it sounds: in school and life, you are generally being told what to do and how to do it. Now is the time to start thinking about what you are good at and what you actually enjoy doing. Think about goals for yourself rather than just wandering aimlessly into every year of high school, studying hard, doing homework, and taking tests; all with no vision of what you are doing it all FOR. Even knowing that you want to go to college and making that your goal is a great starting point!

10th GRADE – HIGH SCHOOL SOPHOMORE

When you reach sophomore year, there is generally a distinct change in 'tone' in your studies. For many students, freshman year was about getting settled into high school, making new friends, handling classes, homework, and tests, possibly playing a sport or being involved in an extracurricular activity and, generally, just trying to balance life. In sophomore year, you may be confronted with options to increase your academic workload with Accelerated Study (AS), Honors, ACP (Advance College Project) classes and/or AP (Advanced Placement) courses, maybe in one or two subjects. These are the things to think about in 10th grade:

IT'S ALL ABOUT THE GRADES
The most important part of your college application is your academic record – and that means grades. If you're aiming for a highly selective college, your grades are scrutinized meticulously and any low grade will limit your options. Consider taking advanced courses if your school offers them.

CONTINUE TAKING CHALLENGING CLASSES
It probably goes without saying that an 'A' in AP English is a more impressive qualification than an 'A' in regular English. The question everyone asks, however, is, "Is a B in an AP class better than an A in a regular class?" Details on grades comparison are included in Chapter 2.

GET ORGANIZED WITH EXTRACURRICULAR ACTIVITIES (OR ACTIVITY)
It is not about the quantity of extracurricular activities you do that will impress colleges, but the quality. Try to find something you love doing and stick with it. Playing trumpet in the marching band for all four years of high school will impress colleges more than a few weeks here and there of different activities. Think of your extracurricular activities as creating a story about yourself: if you are doing something you love, it will come across in the application.

TAKE THE PSAT AND A PRACTICE ACT
Many schools now offer the PSAT (Preliminary Scholastic Aptitude Test) in October of sophomore year and it is a very good idea to take it. Don't worry about the score – the important reason for taking the test is to familiarize yourself with the content and timing to prepare you for the real thing. The same is true for the ACT. If your school doesn't offer practice tests, you might find them offered at a local library. If you can, take one. Once you have results of both tests, you can decide on which one you prefer to concentrate. Factors to consider are:

1) On which test did you get the highest grade?
2) Which one do you like better?

TAKE SAT SUBJECT TEST(S)
These short, one-hour long tests are generally taken in junior and senior years, but there are a number of reasons why they can be taken in sophomore year. If you are taking Chemistry, for example, and you don't think you will go on to take AP Chemistry, it is worth considering taking the Chemistry SAT Subject test at the end of the year in which you have completed the study. Firstly, you will be studying for finals anyway, and secondly, you may never know as much about Chemistry as you do at that point! Taking a SAT subject test is valuable practice in test taking and in understanding formats and managing timing.

TAKE AP EXAMS IF YOU TAKE THE CLASS
If you take an AP course, it is worthwhile taking the AP exam at the end of the year. A score of 4 or 5 (out of 5) is very good and will be an impressive addition to your college application.

GETTING THROUGH IT TOGETHER

GET TO KNOW THE COMMON APPLICATION
With over 800 colleges using the Common Application as the main processing system for applications from students all over the nation and world, it is worthwhile familiarizing yourself with this document as early as possible. The Common App (as it is generally known) provides information on college requirements and deadlines that will help you make decisions about class choices and tests.

START COLLEGE RESEARCH AND VISIT COLLEGES
Even though you may be busy, sophomore year is a good time to start looking at colleges and getting some ideas about what you are looking for in your college experience. A good place to start is to take a walk around colleges near you. Getting a 'feel' for a campus will give you a starting point for your search. You can also take formal tours and learn about how a college works and what type of life you can expect there. Start researching colleges online. You can use the College Visit/Search template in Chapter 3 to keep track of information on each school.

GET ACCESS TO THE COLLEGE BOARD 'COLLEGE HANDBOOK' CATALOG
This guide provides information on every accredited college in the U.S. (2,200 4-year colleges and universities and 1,600 2-year Community Colleges and Technical Schools) and will be indispensable to you when you start creating your college list. Most high school counseling offices will have at least one copy of the latest edition of this catalog. The high school library and local library might also have copies.

PREPARE A RÉSUMÉ
The Résumé is a useful document that you will use over the next few years as:

- The basis document for completing the Activities section of the Common Application and other Applications that require lists of activities and accomplishments;
- A helpful document to hand to your teachers and counselor when requesting letters of recommendation;
- An additional document to submit to colleges (if required or recommended) as part of your college application.

READ, READ, READ
It cannot be stressed enough that the more reading you do, the better your reading, writing, vocabulary, and critical thinking skills will be. These skills are essential skills for college and extremely important in all higher-level classes, particularly English and History. It is also important that you find time to read the news and 'engage' with the world beyond your own. Read the news every morning from a reputable news source online.

PLAN FOR A PRODUCTIVE SUMMER
It's been a busy year and you're tired. Nothing would give you greater pleasure than to relax all summer. But for the serious college applicant, this is not the best way to spend such valuable time. The summer before junior year is when you should:

1. Get a job or internship;
2. Attend a summer program;
3. Attend a college class;
4. Evaluate your academic performance and work on weak areas;
5. Read.

11TH GRADE – HIGH SCHOOL JUNIOR

The college application process really switches into another gear in your junior year. It is really important to get organized (if you are not already!) and stay organized. There will be deadlines and application requirements that need to be met. You don't need to know exactly where you want to apply, but you do need a plan of action. These are the most important things you need to keep working on:

GET ORGANIZED - PUT IT ON PAPER
A paper 'to do' list in plain sight is a reminder of what needs to be done and a record of what has been done. Just like in grade school, achieving those little stars for a job well done, the paper list can be a great source of comfort (that you have everything you need to do written in one place) and pride (you've GOT this!). The templates in this book will help you get started on lists that you can personalize with information that is pertinent to you at any given time throughout the process.

TAKE THE PSAT with NMSQT (National Merit Scholarship Qualifying Test)
Colleges do not see scores on the PSAT, but an excellent score can make you a candidate for the National Merit Scholarship, a rare and prestigious award for U.S. citizens or permanent residents who score within the top 1% of test takers in October of Junior year. Taking the PSAT/NMSQT is good preparation for the real test. Scores from the PSAT can be evaluated against the score ranges of your chosen colleges, giving you a good idea of the work you need to do to prepare for the real thing.

TAKE THE ACT
If you haven't already done so, a good strategy is to take a practice (or real) ACT around the same time as you take the PSAT. You will then be able to compare the tests and decide on which you favor. Before taking a real test, however, please note that, although it is not usual, some schools require a full history of standardized tests you have taken, so if your real ACT score is disappointing, you may have to show that on your application.

KEEP TAKING CHALLENGING CLASSES
In junior year, you want to push yourself to do as well as you possibly can in as many challenging classes as you can handle. If you have access to AP classes, take them, especially in the subjects in which you are interested and/or have done very well in the previous year or two.

KEEP YOUR GRADES UP
It is not enough to take challenging classes without getting good grades in them. If your freshman and/or sophomore grades are not all you hoped they would be, this is the year that you really need to step up your game. Don't wait another minute! And certainly don't wait for senior year. In a sense, junior year is the year that matters most. A downturn in grades in your junior year can be a red flag for college admissions officers.

KEEP ON GOING WITH A FOREIGN LANGUAGE
The requirement for number of years of study of a foreign language differs from school to school. Some require two to three years, and some require four. Be sure to check on the required or recommended number of years of study for the schools in which you are interested.

BE A LEADER
Colleges like to see evidence of some form of leadership, whether in sports, music, or clubs. Taking ownership of an activity demonstrates leadership qualities. Activities such as tutoring peers or younger students, organizing an event, founding a club, or having a role in a fundraising campaign are all evidence that you are responsible and able to work with others.

CONTINUE WITH YOUR COLLEGE RESEARCH
If you've managed to do a little college research in sophomore year and through the rising junior summer, you may already have a good idea about some colleges. However, to enhance your research, it is a good idea to:

- Attend a college fair in your area;
- Visit colleges in which you have particular interest;
- Build a comprehensive College Blueprint (see Chapter 3).

START THINKING ABOUT MAJORS
You don't have to declare a major but many colleges will require you to state an area of academic interest so that they can build a balanced freshman class. Questions to ask yourself as you think about a possible major are:

- What am I good at?
- What classes keep me interested?
- What would I like to know more about?

If you're good at Math, for example, research areas of study in which your skills will be an asset, such as, Economics, Accounting, and/or Business.

IN THE SPRING, TAKE THE SAT and/or THE ACT
If you haven't already done so, take the SAT and/or ACT early in the spring. If you don't get the scores you want, you will have plenty of time to take additional tests. Remember, you only need to choose one test – either the SAT or the ACT – don't waste time studying for both.

IN THE SPRING, MEET WITH YOUR COUNSELOR AND DRAFT A COLLEGE LIST
In this meeting, indicate to your counselor your interests and aspirations and listen carefully to his or her advice. There is no magic number of schools to which you should apply, but it is a good idea to have about 12 to 18 in your first list. For guidance on building a college list, see Chapter 3.

TAKE AP EXAMS AND SAT SUBJECT TESTS
The results of AP exams and SAT Subject tests can indicate to college admissions officers how much you have learned in the period of study to which they relate. Achieving a 4 or 5 in an AP exam is evidence of academic abilities and potential. A 3 in an AP exam will not be considered good enough for college credit perhaps, but you should still indicate it in your application. The fact that you have taken an AP class and the exam is the important element here.

Only a relatively small number of schools actually 'require' SAT Subject tests but over recent years more schools now indicate that they 'recommend' them and/or will evaluate them as part of your application if submitted. These tests are evidence that you have understood material and can perform well in testing situations. Students applying to the more selective schools should consider taking two or three. Unless a school requires them, you do not need to indicate that you have taken these tests on your application.

PREPARING FOR THE COLLEGE APPLICATIONS PROCESS

AT THE END OF THE SCHOOL YEAR, ASK TEACHERS FOR LETTERS OF RECOMMENDATION
As you leave junior year behind, visit two teachers from who you would like letters of recommendation, preferably teachers in core subjects and from a coach if you are an athlete. It is a good idea to give them a copy of your résumé (or email it) so that they have a full 'picture' of you as an individual and not rely only on what they know of you in their class. Your counselor will write a letter automatically, separate from the teachers' recommendations. For information on letters of recommendation, see Chapter 2.

PLAN A PRODUCTIVE SUMMER
This will be a busy summer – or should be! You should aim to find a job, internship, study experience, or volunteer opportunity, or a combination of two or more of these. This is also the time you should plan to write your college application essays. It is strongly recommended that you complete most of your college essays during the summer BEFORE senior year so that you do not have the stress of having to do them at the same time as managing a senior workload.

12TH GRADE – HIGH SCHOOL SENIOR

The first semester of senior year is an extremely important time in the college applications process. If you have followed the guidelines up to this point, you are well prepared for what is ahead. If not, you will need to focus. The things you must do are divided into the months of the senior year, starting several weeks before you even set foot onto campus as a senior.

JUNE/ JULY BEFORE SENIOR YEAR
- Register for August SAT if appropriate;
- Register for the September ACT if appropriate;
- Continue research of colleges and input admission requirements in your college blueprint;
- Create an account in the Common Application and start to familiarize yourself with it;
- Review the Common Application essay prompts and start thinking about which one you want to answer. Make notes where possible – you will find them useful when you come to brainstorming and writing (See Chapter 5);
- Check your senior class schedule to ensure that you are taking all the appropriate classes for your top choice colleges.

AUGUST BEFORE SENIOR YEAR
- Get started on your Common Application essay. Brainstorm and produce an outline; Don't worry about making it perfect at this stage – just get something written down;
- Visit college campuses if you can;
- Add colleges to your list on the Common App and ensure that you leave contact details for every school to be able to contact you;
- Continue to visit campuses and interview with college representatives if possible;
- Collate all the prompts for required college applications writing in one table (See Essay tracker example in Chapter 5);
- Draft a Submissions schedule (see Chapter 6).

SEPTEMBER
- Meet with your high school guidance counselor to discuss colleges;
- Request (or remind, if previously agreed) teachers of letters of recommendation and tell them if you are applying Early Decision (a binding contract) or Early Action (a non-binding contract);

- Attend college visits at your school and introduce yourself to representatives of the colleges you are most interested to attend;
- Indicate your interest in receiving material from the colleges to which you are applying. You can do this with many schools through the Common Application;
- Create a chart of deadlines and required writing. Pay close attention to early decision (binding), early action (non-binding), and preferred action deadlines. Make a paper copy and pin it up it in front of you above your workspace (see Chapter 4). This information is also available on Naviance and on the Common Application website. However, if you are applying to colleges through different applications, it is advisable to create your own list and have all the information in one place;
- If necessary, apply for October ACT exam;
- Keep working on your college essays, especially supplements for the colleges to which you are applying Early Decision and/or Early Action;
- Try to get a leadership position in an extracurricular activity;
- Keep on working to maintain your GPA;
- If you did not do it before, request a copy of your high school transcript and check it for accuracy.

OCTOBER
- Take the SAT or ACT and SAT Subject exams as necessary but be aware that doing this may inhibit you from applying early action to schools with October deadlines;
- Continue to refine your college list. An ideal number is usually 12 or less;
- Complete applications for colleges to which you are applying early decision and/or early action. The earliest submission date for early action and decision schools is 15 October;
- Complete and submit applications to schools with rolling admission policy;
- Continue working on essays and supplements for colleges to which you are applying regular decision. Read every essay out aloud to yourself. When you feel happy with it, ask a parent, counselor, and/or teacher for their feedback. Don't ask for too many opinions;
- Keep track of all application requirements. You can add this information to your college blueprint;
- Research financial aid and scholarships. Ask your parents if their places of employment offer college scholarships for children of employees.

NOVEMBER
- Last chance! Register for the December SAT or ACT if appropriate;
- Take the November SAT or ACT if appropriate;
- Keep up your grades. 'Senioritis' is real and you can get easily distracted, especially if you already have some offers from colleges. A dip in grades could have disastrous consequences (some colleges may rescind offers if they see this);
- Ensure that you have submitted all components of your applications for schools with a 30 November deadline (e.g., The University of California and California State Schools);
- Continue to research scholarships. Some private schools automatically consider a student's application for scholarship opportunities and others have separate essays for consideration for scholarships. If interested in scholarships, make sure that you complete all required essays within the application for the appropriate college.

DECEMBER – JANUARY
- Complete your application for regular admission;
- Ensure that you send (or have sent) your test scores sent to all colleges that require them;
- Confirm that your letters of recommendation have been sent and received;

- Submit the FAFSA (Free Application for Financial Aid);
- If you are accepted to a school through early decision, you are committed to attend that school. Follow directions carefully, submit all required forms, and immediately withdraw your applications from the other schools to which you applied;
- Have mid-year grades sent to the colleges to which you have applied;
- Keep track of all materials required by schools. Keep an eye out for emails from your schools. If required, create an account on the college portal;
- Continue to research scholarships. Also, keep an eye open for applications for scholarship and/or honors programs from the colleges to which you have applied;
- Confirm that every college to which you applied has received your application. If you have not received a confirmation of receipt, contact the college admissions office immediately.

FEBRUARY – MARCH
- If you submitted the FAFSA, you should receive the Student Aid Report (SAR). Check it very carefully - errors can cost you thousands of dollars;
- If you are applying to schools with rolling admissions, get those done now – even if they have a much later deadline. Places fill up quickly and an early application can be advantageous;
- Talk to your teacher/counselor and make sure you are registered for AP exams for which you are working;
- Keep up your grades. Colleges do not look favorably on a student who loses focus and can sometimes revoke an offer of admission;
- When acceptance letters arrive, compare financial aid offers and scholarship/honors opportunities and, if possible, visit campuses before making a decision;
- Continue to apply for scholarships, however they are presented to you (via a school or external body/institution).

APRIL
- Yes, I'll keep on saying it: Keep your grades up!
- Keep track of all acceptances, deferrals, waitlists, and scholarship offers. This information can be added to your Submission Schedule (See Chapter 6);
- If waitlisted at a favorite or favored school, consider writing a letter to the admissions office to update them of your accomplishments since you sent your application; Likewise, if you have been rejected from your favorite school, you might want to consider a last ditch attempt for consideration by updating them with your grades and activities (See Chapter 6);
- If you get the chance, make final campus visits and/or overnight visits at your favorite of the schools to which you have been accepted (See Chapter 3).

MAY
- Accept your offer to your chosen college;
- If you have absolutely ruled out any colleges that accepted you, notify them. This is not necessary, but it is courteous and, even more important, it will open up places for other applicants for whom this college might be a first choice.

1.2 TO DO LIST FOR JUNIORS AND SENIORS

It is useful to keep a 'To Do' list in your workspace so that you can keep track of everything that needs to be done within senior and junior years, as below:

GETTING THROUGH IT TOGETHER

COLLEGE PLANNING 'TO DO' LIST
JUNIOR YEAR - FIRST SEMESTER- OCTOBER
Take PSAT (score from this test is evaluated for National Merit Scholarship)
DECEMBER
Take a practice (or official) ACT
JUNIOR YEAR - SECOND SEMESTER - JANUARY
Meet your High School College Counselor
Review your PSAT and ACT results - evaluate your scores - register for test of choice
Start to build a résumé
FEBRUARY
If available to you, learn to use Naviance
Begin college search - research colleges you are thinking about - make a preliminary list
Start to build a college list with admissions criteria - know what you're working for!
Arrange visits to colleges in spring break
MARCH
If possible, visit some schools over spring break
Prepare for SAT or ACT
APRIL
Discuss with counselor standardized test plans and Senior year classes
Attend College Fair
MAY
Take appropriate SAT tests and AP exams
Finalize your preliminary college list
If you might play Division I or II sports, register with NCAA Eligibility Center
Ask teachers for letters of recommendation (and give them your résumé)
JUNE
If planning to do so, take SAT subject tests
Plan summer college visits - tours, information session, and interviews. Make appointments and try to visit with professors and/or coaches where possible.
SUMMER (JULY - AUGUST)
Create an account on the Common Application and complete generic information
Start writing essays and supplements
Register for SAT, ACT and/or SAT subject tests in October and/or November as needed
Research colleges and continue to refine your list

PREPARING FOR THE COLLEGE APPLICATIONS PROCESS

SENIOR YEAR - FIRST SEMESTER - AUGUST-SEPTEMBER
Meet with counselor and discuss early application and early decision plans
Confirm 2 teacher recommendations (and enter names in Naviance)
Complete FERPA Agreement on Naviance
Ensure your class selection meets requirements for high school graduation, for college systems, and NCAA if relevant
Arrange interviews where applicable
Take the ACT if applicable
OCTOBER
Retake SAT or SAT subject tests, send scores to four colleges for free
Financial Aid applicants should file a CSS Profile registration form (see Financial Aid section)
Confirm dates for Early Action' (non-binding) applications and submit at least one week before deadline (allows time to send additional material if required).
If applying 'Early Decision' (binding), ensure that you have all materials ready and submit at least one week before deadline
Complete essays and supplements for Early Decision and/or Early Action colleges
NOVEMBER
Ensure that transcripts are sent to all your schools
Look out for messages from each college and, when required, create an account on each portal.
DECEMBER
If you receive an admission offer from your Early Decision college, send an acceptance note and withdraw from all other colleges to which you have applied.
SENIOR YEAR - SECOND SEMESTER - JANUARY
Submit FAFSA forms within deadline
FEBRUARY - MARCH - APRIL
Keep an eye on correspondence from colleges
Write scholarship essays if offered
Create an acceptance list - keep track of offers with details of scholarships, honors programs, etc.
MAY
Send acceptance letter to your chosen school
Send polite email declining all other colleges to which you were accepted
JUNE
Graduate from High School and get ready for college!

1.3 GET TO KNOW YOURSELF

The following questions will help you start thinking about who you are and what you value. Honest, thoughtful responses will:

- Help you find colleges that are right for you by matching your aspirations and abilities with a college's requirements and preferences;
- Prepare you for questions you may be asked on applications essays and in interviews;
- Help you present yourself effectively to the colleges of your choice;
- Help you take an honest, realistic look at yourself in the college application process.

	Your Personality and Relationships
1	How would someone who knows you well describe you?
2	What would that person say are your best qualities?
3	What would that person say are your shortcomings?
4	In what ways have you changed in your high school years?
5	Which relationships are most important to you and why?
6	Describe your 'best' friends. Why do you feel close to them?
7	Do you feel you are easily influenced by the people you care about?
8	How important to you are rewards, approval, and recognition?
9	How do you respond to pressure, competition, or challenge?
10	How do you respond to criticism, disappointment, or failure?
11	How would you describe your family and home?
12	How have they influenced your way of thinking?
13	How have your interests and abilities been acknowledged or limited by them?
14	What do your parents and others expect of you?
15	How have those expectations influenced the standards and goals you set for yourself?
16	To what pressures have you felt it necessary to conform?
	The World Around You
1	What is the most controversial issue you have encountered in recent years?
2	Why does the issue concern you?
3	How have you reacted to the issue?
4	What is your opinion on the issue?
5	Have you encountered people who think and act differently from you?
6	What viewpoints/behaviors have challenged you the most?
7	How did you respond?
8	What did you learn about yourself and others?
9	What concerns you most about the world around you?
10	If you could, what would you change about the world? Where would you start?

PREPARING FOR THE COLLEGE APPLICATIONS PROCESS

	Your Education
1	What are your academic interests?
2	Which classes have you enjoyed the most? Why?
3	Which classes have been most difficult for you? Why?
4	What do you choose to learn when you can learn on your own?
5	How do you learn best? What methods of teaching and/or style of teacher engage you most?
6	In what areas do you feel most prepared for college?
7	In what areas do you feel least prepared for college?
8	Do you feel your academic record and/or SAT scores are reflective of you academic potential?
9	What do you feel are the best measures of YOUR potential for college?
10	Are there any circumstances that have interfered with your academic performance?
	Your Activities and Interests
1	What activities do you most enjoy outside of classes and other responsibilities?
2	Which activities have meant the most to you? Why?
3	Looking back, would you have made different choices?
4	What would you consider your most significant contribution to your school? your community?
5	What are you really good at?
6	What activity would you like to try?
7	What activities do you do with your family that you enjoy?
8	Where in the world would you like to travel?
9	Where do you feel happy? Relaxed? Energized?
10	What is your ideal form of relaxation?
	Your Goals and Values
1	What aspects of your high school years have been most meaningful to you?
2	If you could do it again, would you do anything differently?
3	What does 'success' mean to you?
4	Are you satisfied with your accomplishments to date?
5	What do you want to accomplish in the years ahead?
6	Which of your talents would you most like to develop?
7	What would you most like to change about yourself?
8	Is there anything you have ever secretly wanted to do or be?
9	What are the three most important things in your life?
10	Is there a profession you admire or would like to learn more about?

1.4 TAKE CONTROL

To be as effective and productive as possible, it's important that you get organized and prepare yourself for the work ahead. As you see from the college timeline, whatever grade you are in at high school, it is not too early to be thinking about college. Even if it all seems a long way off, try at least to commit yourself to three things:

FOCUS – more than any other time in your life, you are in control of your goal(s). Keep in mind that you – and only you – are responsible for getting the grades you need to apply to the schools you want to attend.

PREPARATION – you will have lots of help from parents, teachers, and counselors in preparing you for what lies ahead but, ultimately, it is your responsibility to do your best work at all times. And, if your results are not as you wish, don't lose heart; just be better prepared for the next test, exam, or assignment. Make sure that everything you do is your best work. It all counts.

BELIEF IN YOURSELF – many of the things ahead are not easy but, with realistic confidence and belief in yourself and your abilities, you can achieve your dreams. Take a deep breath; think about what you have to do, and a goal you wish to achieve.

The process is about setting out a plan of how to approach it. One of the ways to think about it is to understand that you – and you alone - have the POWER to make this happen. I've used POWER as an acronym to break down the process like this:

	Using your POWER to get into college
Prepare	Think about what you want - set realistic goals
	Take challenging classes
	Be your own best advocate
	Sleep
	Take pride in your work and your work ethic
	Take a leadership class
Organize	Set up a study space – have all the things you need and keep it tidy
	Allot time to each project
	Keep up with the workload - don't procrastinate
	Keep your backpack and/or locker organized
Work	Find ways to 'get in the zone'
	Time your homework
	Be careful of collaboration
	Participate in class - in a positive way
	Get to know your teachers - they want you to succeed
	Be proud of yourself - you are working towards an important goal
Evaluate	Be your own best guide - you 'know' better than anyone what you need to do
	If you need help, ask
	Go to teachers' after office hours for help
	Get study buddies - test each other
Repeat	Yes, keep on doing it!
	Set aside time to look over your work
	Ask yourself if you are doing your best work

1.5 STUDY TIPS

Work/Study Effectiveness Self-Evaluation

If you feel you could be more focused and productive, it is worthwhile evaluating how you study. Below is a self-evaluation exercise that you should complete during and after a study session:

Work/Study Effectiveness Self Evaluation	
Column 1 (fill out during work/study session)	**Column 2 (fill out after work/study session)**
Date: Where: Start time: Study conditions (e.g. home, library, with friends?)	Were the place, time, and conditions the best possible? Could I improve anything? (e.g. study alone, no music, study with friends, wear glasses, use alarm clock?)
Total time I am going to study:	For how long did I actually study?
Number of breaks I intend to take?	Number of breaks I took? (Including time on social media, messaging friends, getting a snack, etc.)
Approximate times of breaks: Length of breaks:	Did I stick to the break time? If not, what do I need to do? (e.g. time my breaks, elongate my study time, remove distractions, etc.?)
Interruptions that occurred: Type of interruption Length of interruption 1 2 3 4 5	How could I prevent these interruptions?
Time finished: Total time worked:	ACTUAL time spent studying:
What did I do well?	Why did I do better in this session?
What prevents me from doing better?	To do better in weaker areas, I need to: What can I do to improve?

Organize a Work Space
You will work more efficiently if you have SPACE. You need somewhere to work that is easily accessible and comfortable (you'll be spending some time here) and, most of all, quiet. If your space is your bedroom, try and find a corner that you will use solely for working. I know that many students like to lay on their beds to study, but I have found that when I ask them how effective a study habit this really is, they will often admit that it's actually not that comfortable and makes it far too easy to doze off or lose concentration. Once you move to a dedicated space with a desk or table, students admit that they start to understand how a simple thing such as WHERE they study can have such a huge impact on their productivity.

If finding a space at home is just not possible or if you would prefer to work anywhere but home, why not find somewhere you do like? The local library can be a really good place: quiet, yet full of students like you who have something to do. Use this time to do what you have to do, and force yourself to shut off from all social media.

Some students like to work together, taking little breaks along the way. This may not sound productive but it can be very effective for students for a number of reasons:

- They like to see how other students work;
- They like being asked their opinions;
- They like discussing aspects of the applications and essays;
- They don't want to be seen to be the one slacking in their work;
- They are all working to a common goal.

Use an Alarm Clock
Using an alarm clock when studying is a helpful technique to stay focused and on track: it helps you to *know* time. That may sound strange, but it is actually amazing how few students really understand what five minutes *feels* like. Just try it: don't do anything but watch the clock for five minutes as you boil an egg. It seems *forever!*

When you start your homework or a study session, turn off your phone and anything else that you know is a distraction and set the alarm for, say, 30 minutes. Do nothing but work until the alarm goes off. After a few sessions, you may find that, because you only have a defined amount of time and you know that it will be over soon, you are more focused and productive.

1.6 NOTES FOR STUDENTS WITH LEARNING DIFFERENCES

According to the National Center for Learning Disabilities, approximately one in five American children have difficulty with learning or attention. The Individuals with Disabilities Education Act (IDEA) defines a learning disability (also referred to as learning difference or learning difficulty) as:

> "A disorder in one or more of the basic psychological processes involved in understanding or in using language, spoken or written, which may manifest itself in an imperfect ability to think, speak, read, write, spell, or to do Mathematical calculations."

Learning differences (also referred to as difficulties and disabilities) have nothing to do with a person's intelligence, IQ, or creativity and many individuals with learning differences achieve success because they have unique ways of seeing the world and of applying their knowledge in interesting and creative ways. However, a learning disability can be very hard on a teen's self-esteem, especially in high school and the lead up to college, which can affect their their mood, behavior, and motivation. The main types of learning differences include:

- Dyslexia: Trouble with reading and comprehension (the most common learning disability);
- Dysgraphia: Difficulty writing down thoughts, trouble with grammar;
- Dyscalculia: Problems with numbers and Math skills, including making change and telling time;
- Dyspraxia: Challenges with motor tasks, including hand-eye coordination and balance;
- Auditory Processing Disorder: Difficulty translating sounds into coherent thoughts;
- Processing Disorder: Difficulty translating images into meaningful information.

The IDEA also classifies other behavioral disorders as learning disabilities, including:

- Attention deficit hyperactivity disorder (ADD): Includes symptoms of inattention, distractibility, and poor working memory;
- Attention deficit hyperactivity disorder (ADHD): Includes symptoms such as inattentiveness, hyperactivity and impulsiveness;
- Autism Spectrum Disorder (ASD) (also known as Autism): Refers to a broad range of conditions characterized by challenges with social skills, repetitive behaviors, speech and nonverbal communication;
- Asperger syndrome (AS) (also known as Asperger's): Refers to a developmental disorder characterized by difficulties in social interaction and nonverbal communication and restricted and repetitive patterns of behavior and interests.

A student can 'hide' or not even know that they have a learning difference for many years until they reach high school and are put under pressure of long hours of homework and, specifically, the extreme conditions of standardized tests. There are a number of 'signs' that may indicate a learning difference, including:

- Extreme difficulty, dislike, or delay in writing and/or reading;
- Withdrawal or aggressive behavior;
- Having a hard time comprehending and organizing information;
- Frustration or apathy toward school and classes;
- Sloppy, disorganized schoolwork, and disorganization in general;
- Problems with Math skills;
- Poor memory;
- Difficulty in understanding inference and conjecture;
- Trouble paying attention and following directions;
- Poor coordination;
- Difficulty with concepts related to time;
- Difficulty in expressing themselves.

A student with some of these symptoms does not necessarily have a learning difference but, if symptoms continue or worsen, it is advisable that they be assessed by an appropriate registered Learning Differences specialist. For the student with a learning difference who wishes to go to college, it is especially important that he or she be assessed as early in the process as possible so that they can apply for help at school through the Individualized Education Programs (IEPs) and for accommodations (such as extra time on tests and exams) on the ACT and SAT standardized tests.

Students with learning disabilities will be doing exactly the same process as outlined in this book, and it is important to start the college process early. Obtaining accommodations for students with documented disabilities can take time. In order to enroll in the specialized programs for learning differences, it is likely that the student will need to complete an Eligibility Form of some kind and provide evidence of the learning difference by way of a report from a doctor and/or specialist. A high school counselor will be able to advise you on the exact documentation you will need. Starting to 'casually' look at schools online or in various publications as early as sophomore year is a good time to start: the sooner you have some idea of the schools you might want to attend and of the requirements for admission, the sooner you will be able to work towards making college a reality.

1.6.1. Learning Differences at College

All colleges in the US are required to have a disabilities office, which is meant to help accommodate students with different needs. While disability offices can be helpful when it comes to logistical concerns, some students need more of a supportive structure in place in order for them to feel comfortable. It is therefore important that you research schools very carefully to find the one that fits your needs. A group of schools that go above and beyond the official guidelines in supporting students with learning differences offer a variety of supportive programs, often operated by learning specialists who are trained in working with students who have different needs. Examples of supportive services, programs, and procedures include:

- Weekly meetings with a counselor;
- Reduced course load;
- Extra tutoring support;
- Special curricula;
- On-campus learning specialists;
- Individual meetings with educators;
- Transitional summer programs;
- Specialty workshops.

Colleges offer different combinations of the above support services, according to needs. Not all of the schools that offer enhanced services with learning differences will be suitable for all students with learning disabilities: some offer very high levels of structure and support, whereas others may offer regular check-ins to make sure you're on track. It may be helpful to think about how much support you need before you begin your college search. It is important to remember that virtually all of the schools with the most advanced and supportive programs for students with learning disabilities charge an additional fee on top of tuition costs if the department is embedded within a college. It is also important to remember that, generally, college and learning disability program are separate entities and you need to apply to each separately.

The medium-to-large size colleges that offer the best programs are listed below. These are good choices for the student who wants to have a typical college experience and the additional support of a specialized program:

American University	University of Arizona - Tucson
DePaul University	University of Connecticut
Northeastern University	University of Denver
Rochester Institute of Technology	University of Iowa

PREPARING FOR THE COLLEGE APPLICATIONS PROCESS

For students who prefer a smaller college campus, the following small-to-medium size schools offer excellent support for students with learning differences:

- Augsburg College
- Curry College
- Fairleigh Dickinson University
- Lesley University
- Lynn University
- Marist College
- Mercyhurst College
- Mitchell College

There are a few schools that are dedicated to support of students with learning differences. They are mostly smaller colleges that offer customized levels of support and structure and are experienced in helping students with learning disabilities balance their academics, work, and personal lives:

Beacon College offers Associate and Bachelor degrees exclusively to students with learning disabilities and attention deficit disorders. Beacon's overall graduation rate is 76%, which surpasses the national average graduation rate for students with learning disabilities. The college's support services include a Center for Student Success (with trained learning specialists and tutors), a Math lab, and a writing center.

Landmark College is dedicated to helping students who learn differently (e.g. students with learning disabilities, attention deficit disorders, or dyslexia). Support services that the college offers include:

- Academic advising and coaching;
- Centers for academic support;
- Counseling;
- Specialty summer programs, to ease the transition into college.

A student with learning differences should get as much information about specialized programs as possible to get a better idea of fit and compatibility. Visit campuses, talk to current students, and consider if program offerings would give you the appropriate level of support for your needs. It is helpful to keep notes on each school you research and visit so that you can compare them when the times comes. Many of the schools with specialized learning programs require you to submit an application to the learning disabilities program in addition to the regular college application. You may also have to submit further documentation, including diagnostic tests, psychological evaluations, or letters from educators. Give yourself plenty of time to complete these applications. You can still apply (and be eligible for) financial aid and scholarships, but enrolling in some of these programs could potentially add thousands of dollars to your costs each year. Federal grants and loans can help make up some of the costs of these specialized programs and you should research these for the most up-to-date information. **The following resources are helpful:**

- The K & W Guide to Colleges for Students with Learning Disabilities or Attention Deficit Disorder by Kravets and Wax, is an indispensable resource for students with learning disabilities. It provides advice from specialists, admission requirements, and strategies for finding the right program for each student's needs. It includes 330 school profiles and information on another 1,000 schools.

- Peterson's Colleges With Programs for Students With Learning Disabilities or Attention Deficit Disorders by Charles T. Mangrum and Stephen S. Strichart, highlights over 750 programs at two- and four-year colleges.

- Khan Academy is an online service that provides free courses in Math, Science, history, art, and computer Sciences. It has over 6 million users each month. It simplifies the course material and makes it easy to learn.

Learning Support Centers or Disabled Student Services Offices are the best places to get first-hand information on a school's program and the guidance and support they offer. These programs are often in great demand and it is important to start your research early and learn as much as possible. Suggested questions to ask are:

- What tests are required?
- Can any high school courses be waived?
- Is there an extra fee to participate in the program?
- How many staff members are available?
- Is extra help available for tutoring and other support?
- Are diagnostic tests available?
- Is Assistive Technology available? (Kurzeweil Reader, voice-activated software)
- Are the following allowed for exams - Calculator, computer, electronic texts, extended time, oral exams, note takers?
- Is a Learning Disability specialist available?
- Are professional tutors available?
- Should I mention my disability in my college application?

For additional information, the following resources are helpful:

www.ldonline.org - The official website for the Coordinated Campaign for Learning Disabilities.
www.ldanatl.org - The Learning Disabilities Association.
www.ncld.org - The National Center for Learning Disabilities.
www.perc-schwabfdn.org - Parents and Educators Resource Center PERC founded by the Charles and Helen Schwab Foundation.
www.collegemagazine.com - Well-researched lists of schools that offer support to students with learning differences and minority groups.
www.collegeboard.org - College Board Services for Students with Disabilities (SSD) - Accommodations for PSAT, SAT, SAT Subject tests, and AP examinations.
www.actstudent.org - "Students with Disabilities" - Accommodations for ACT.
www.ncld.org - National Center for Learning Disabilities.
www.ld.org/awards/afscholarinfo.cfm - Anne Ford Scholarship.

1.7   PARENT POINTER – HELPING YOUR TEEN ON THEIR JOURNEY TO COLLEGE

The college applications process is not just a transition for students; it is a huge transition for parents too. No matter what advice parents are given about letting their teen take control of the college applications process themselves, parents need to be involved. Being involved does not mean 'helicopter parenting' (hovering over your child waiting to do everything for them and solve their every problem) or having a 'tiger mom' mentality (ensuring that every single moment of every single day is taken up with intellectual and academic pursuit). It's about listening to your child, offering them sound advice, and helping them make important decisions about their future.

Just at a time when you all need to communicate, however, teens may go through changes in their behavior and moods. Mood swings, withdrawal from family activities, obsessive concern for their appearance, procrastination, and short tempers, are just some of the behavioral changes that many parents need to deal with. Parents may also experience a change in their own behavior as they experience a sense of loss or abandonment as their teen makes their first steps to independence. Together, these changes create opportunities for miscommunication and misunderstandings, which can disrupt and distress the family as a whole.

KNOW WHAT'S GOING ON
Most teens are fearful about the future and talking about college brings them to the stark reality that their whole life is about to change. Some hide their fear by avoiding any conversation about it which can be upsetting to a parent who wants to be involved and can't even mention the word, "college" without a negative reaction. Some may tell their parents that they have the college process under control. You should know, however, that it is unlikely that they do.

The best way to to be of help is to know what is going on and what your teen is going through. Yet, here lies the dilemma: Through college preparation systems such as Naviance, parents now have access to their teen's grades on a day-by-day basis: the B in a history quiz or the F on a Chemistry assignment are there for them to see. It can be an ongoing nightmare for the student whose parents want to discuss every single grade and then warn them that the B- is 'not good enough to get into college.' In situations like this, parents think that they are 'advising,' 'counseling,' 'guiding,' or 'encouraging' and, very often, that's exactly what they are doing. However, during the college applications process – and in fact in most conversations to do with college – well-intentioned parental wisdom gets 'lost in translation' and is invariably construed by the tetchy teenager as 'nagging.' To avoid making every conversation about college, some parents and their teens have found it helpful to arrange 'college catch-up' sessions on an arranged regular basis. The advantages of this is that the catch-up session can be as often as you both like, and it allows you both time to organize your thoughts and questions.

HELP CREATE A GOOD ENVIRONMENT
It is helpful to think about the college applications process as a 'project.' The foundation of success for any project is good planning within an environment that is conducive to success. Ask your teen about the kind of environment they want for their study space. Many students tell me they study on their bed but also admit to frequently dozing off or watching a show on their laptop. A dedicated study space – with a desk, chair, and lamp – is preferable and may help them stay focused and organized. Wherever they decide they would like to study, you can help organize the space to make it their own.

Many students tell me they sometimes feel overwhelmed with schoolwork and activities. Sleep and nutritious food can help them stay strong. So many teens stay up late and fall into bed completely exhausted. The next day they are tired and cannot concentrate. Helping them instigate a bedtime routine is not easy, but can be gently encouraged. Quiet time (remember giving that when they were five years' old!) will help them wind down. It's helpful to avoid conversations about school, grades, and college late in the evening. Some students find the alarm clock study technique (see Study Skills section) quite helpful in giving them extra time to watch a show perhaps and, more importantly, to sleep. Ending the day with a cup of hot chocolate or chamomile tea can also be a good 'signal' for bed.

Many teenagers eat 'on the run' and grab whatever they can that is quick and easy. Healthy foods such as vegetables and fruit may be the last thing they choose (unless they are vegetarian!) If your teen is picky or not making healthy food choices, try to incorporate healthy foods into the foods they do like, such as dicing or mashing vegetables into a spaghetti sauce, soup, or chili. Asking for their help in the kitchen, or getting them to prepare a meal or two, can also spark interest in preparing nutritious food.

If your teen deliberately avoids eating and if you have any concerns about their eating behavior, it is wise to get help as soon as possible. Anorexia, bulimia, and other food-related issues are serious conditions and your teen needs professional help in dealing with them.

MONEY
Talking about money with your teen, explaining what a budget is, giving them a weekly allowance and guidelines for spending it, and setting up a savings account with them will all help your child understand the value of money. Parents are often fundamental to the financing of their child's college experience or to advising them about taking on financial obligations. It is advisable that you talk to your teen about college costs, the financial resources that are available to them, and the contribution you expect from them.

HELPING A TEEN WITH A LEARNING DIFFERENCE
If a teen is diagnosed with a learning difference, it can be both a liberating and traumatic experience for them: Liberating because they now know why they can't finish the test or understand Calculus, and traumatic because they now have to catch up and, potentially, learn new ways to 'learn' (note-taking systems, reading programs, etc.) Parents, families, and teachers can support a teen with a Learning Difference by:

- *Remain sensitive and compassionate: remember that your teen is struggling;*
- *Focus on strengths;*
- *Help teens recognize and appreciate their strengths. Every teen has something they're good at, whether it's art, writing, sports, or being a good friend to others. Whatever their strength(s), encourage them and give them opportunities to shine;*
- *Create routines and structure;*
- *Help them organize their 'stuff.' Clear a space for them, provide storage boxes, and help them with planning and structuring their day, studies, and activities;*
- *Give them opportunities to speak for themselves in getting what they want and need;*
- *Help them with decisions, such as college choices and major selection (if appropriate);*
- *Encourage them to do the things they love and give them ideas on how their strengths will be relevant, important, and valued in the outside world;*
- *Seek expert guidance and learn everything you can about your teen's condition. Talk to professionals in the fields of education, behavior, and mental health.*

KEEP IT IN PERSPECTIVE
If your son or daughter intends to go to college, they are embarking on an exciting journey to the next phase of their lives. Please note that I say "the next phase" and not "the most important phase" of their lives. It is important to always keep this thought in perspective: College is a stepping-stone, not a destination. The keys to success in the college applications process are to keep an open mind and value this time with them.

Children have never been very good at listening to their elders, but they have never failed to imitate them."

— James Baldwin

CHAPTER 2

ACADEMIC PREPARATION

"If we all did the things we are capable of doing, we would literally astound ourselves."

— Thomas Edison

ACADEMIC PREPARATION

2.1 ACADEMIC PROFILE

You need to know EXACTLY what type of student you are in order to start thinking about college. An Academic Profile will give you an honest picture of your academic achievements and help you establish realistic goals. An Academic Profile is a record of all your academic achievements and grades during high school so far. Having all this information in one place will be useful when you start building your résumé and filling out college applications. From the profile you will be able to see your academic strengths and weaknesses and also any gaps in your curriculum, which will help you plan the classes you need. Below are samples of Academic Profile and Class/GPA Profile templates:

Academic Profile			
	Subject	*Grades/Scores*	*Date*
GPA			
GPA - 9th grade	1st semester		
	2nd semester		
GPA 10th grade	1st semester		
	2nd semester		
GPA - 11th grade	1st semester		
	2nd semester		
GPA - 12th grade	1st semester		
	2nd semester		
ADVANCED CLASSES			
Advanced Placement (AP)	AP 1		
	AP 2		
	AP 3		
	AP 4		
Honors Classes	Subject 1		
	Subject 2		
College Courses/ Other	Subject 1		
	Subject 2		
STANDARDIZED TESTS			
PSAT 1 (9th)			
PSAT 2 (10th)			
SAT	1st		
	2nd		
Practice ACT			
ACT	1st		
	2nd		
SAT Subject tests	Subject 1		
	Subject 2		
	Subject 3		

GETTING THROUGH IT TOGETHER

Classes/GPA Profile							
Freshman - 1st semester				**Freshman - 2nd semester**			
Class	Subject	Grade	Calc for GPA	Class	Subject	Grade	Calc for GPA
			GPA				GPA
Sophomore - 1st semester				**Sophomore - 2nd semester**			
Class	Subject	Grade	Calc for GPA	Class	Subject	Grade	Calc for GPA
			GPA				GPA
Junior - 1st semester				**Junior - 2nd semester**			
Class	Subject	Grade	Calc for GPA	Class	Subject	Grade	Calc for GPA
			GPA				GPA
Senior - 1st semester				**Senior - 2nd semester**			
Class	Subject	Grade	Calc for GPA	Class	Subject	Grade	Calc for GPA
			GPA				GPA

ACADEMIC PREPARATION

2.1.1 GPA (GRADE POINT AVERAGE)

A grade point average, or GPA as it is more commonly called, is a number representing the average value of the accumulated final grades earned in courses over time. GPA is calculated by dividing the total number of accumulated final grades by the number of grades awarded. This calculation results in a Mathematical mean—or average—of all final grades. The most common form of GPA is based on a 0 to 4.0 scale, where:

A = 4.0
B = 3.0
C = 2.0
D = 1.0
F = 0

In this scenario, a 4.0 represents a "perfect" GPA: a student having earned straight As in every course. Schools may also assign partial points for "plus" or "minus" letter grades, such as a 3.7 for an A–, a 3.3 for a B+, and so on. GPAs may be calculated at the end of a course, semester, or grade level, and a "cumulative GPA" represents an average of all final grades individual students earned from the time they first enrolled in a school to the completion of their education.

In some schools, a weighted-grade system is used to calculate a GPA, whereby students are given numerical advantage for grades earned in higher-level courses, such as honors classes, Advanced Placement (AP) classes, International Baccalaureate, or other more challenging classes. In weighted-grade systems, an A in a higher-level course might be awarded a 4.5 or 5.0, for example, while an A in a lower-level course is awarded a 4.0. Weighted-grade systems vary widely in design and methodology and it is therefore important that you know how this works in your school. A student's GPA is often used to determine academic honors, such as honor roll, class rank, or Latin honors (summa, magna, and cum laude). In public schools, grading systems and GPA scales may vary significantly from one school or school district to the next. When investigating or reporting on grading systems, class rank, or other academic honors, it is important to determine how grades and GPAs are calculated and what evaluation criteria was used to measure academic performance and award grades.

GPAs have been one of several major factors used by colleges, postsecondary programs, and employers to assess a student's overall academic record. It is an important indicator of your success in high school and it is to your benefit to work towards achieving the best grades you can to ensure that you have a GPA that is representative of your hard work and academic abilities. Unlike standardized tests that represent the ability to take a test on a particular day, your GPA says a great deal about your academic abilities, perseverance, commitment, and potential for further academic success.

GPA is also used often used to determine class rank, a term that refers to the hierarchical ranking of students based on academic performance, which is expressed in numerical order (first, second, third, top ten, etc.) or as percentiles (top ten percent, top twenty-five percent, etc.). Class rank is typically determined at the end of middle school or high school, and it is used to determine academic honors such as valedictorian (first in the class) and salutatorian (second in the class). While schools do not typically make an entire set of rankings for a graduating class public, it is quite common for schools to publicly announce and celebrate top-ranked students, particular those who end up in the "top ten" or top-tenth percentile. Colleges often use class rank as one component of evaluation of an applicant.

For automatic GPA calculation, use: https://gpacalculator.net/high-school-gpa-calculator/

2.1.2 HIGH SCHOOL CLASSES REQUIRED FOR COLLEGE

You must ensure that you are on track for fulfilling all the classes required for completing your high school diploma and taking enough of the right classes as prerequisite for applying to college. The following classes are a guideline as to those requirements, but you should check with your high school counselor to make sure that you are on target:

ENGLISH: 4 years
This includes courses in which your study writing and courses in which you read literature.
You need to be able to write well in nearly all careers. Use your English classes to read, analyze, and develop strong communication skills.

MATH: 3-4 years
It is advisable to take FOUR years of Math classes. Students who take Math in every year of high school are more successful in college than students who take only three years. It is advisable not to skip a year of Math in high school because you will lose momentum. Your Math classes should include three or four of the following classes, taken in this order:

- Pre-Algebra
- Algebra
- Geometry
- Algebra II and/or Trigonometry
- Pre Calculus
- Calculus

SCIENCE: 3-4 years
Take three to four years of laboratory Science classes. You will have the strongest background if you have taken at least one year each of:

- Biology
- Chemistry
- Physics

SOCIAL STUDIES: 2 years minimum
Most colleges require a minimum of two years of social studies. The majority of college freshmen studied World History and US History in high school. Other social studies options include:

- US Government
- Sociology
- Geography
- Psychology
- Micro Economics
- Macro Economics

FOREIGN LANGUAGE: 2-4 years

ACADEMIC PREPARATION

The general requirement for a foreign language for most colleges has been 2 to 3 years. However, many of the selective schools now 'recommend' 3 to 4 years, and some 'require' 4 years study at high school level. When you are selecting classes, it's a good idea to research exact requirements.

ARTS
Colleges often require one year of visual or performing arts prior to admission. Again, it is a good idea to check the exact requirements for each of the colleges in which you are interested.

2.1.3 ADVANCED CLASSES IN HIGH SCHOOL

Beyond the core curriculum classes that you are required to take in order to graduate high school there are more challenging classes that you should consider and discuss with your counselor and relevant teacher. Advanced classes are opportunities to challenge yourself, immerse yourself in a subject or subjects in which you are interested, and make maximum impact on your college applications. You should think about taking these classes if:

- You have good grades in the subject, and/or;
- You like a subject, and/or;
- You have your mind set on a professional pathway that require the highest grades in specific subjects at high school level, e.g. Sciences and Math for Medicine, and Math and Physics for Engineering, and/or;
- You already have an idea of a college you would like to attend and/or the program you want and you must fulfill particular requirements.

In a situation where you have a good grade in a class, but don't particularly like the class, ask yourself *why* you don't like the class and evaluate if a different teacher, a group of smarter students, or simply a different time of the day might improve it for you. The point is, try not to let external factors deter you from achieving your potential. High schools may offer advanced classes, the most common of which are:

Advanced Placement (AP) Classes
AP courses consist of advanced subject matter taught at a faster pace than regular courses. The variety and number of AP classes offered in high schools varies considerably. Students in these classes complete advanced, college-level coursework. At the end of each course, they take a standardized test, the score of which is an indicator of the student's knowledge of the subject matter. A score of 4 or 5 is good for evaluation purposes and, in the past, may have been sufficient for credit. Now, many colleges no longer offer credit for AP classes and use them only as a way to allow a student to bypass introductory courses. This is particularly important to consider when considering taking Science and Math classes. The college may provide general credit, but the engineering department may not accept them as part of the degree requirement. When considering AP classes, remember:

- Selective colleges expect students to challenge themselves and will be looking for evidence that you have done so, which means that you should think about taking Advanced Placement and Honors classes in subjects in which you feel confident;

- You report grades from your freshman, sophomore, and junior years. It will enhance your application to have AP and/or honors courses on your transcript. If you plan to take advanced classes, do not wait until senior year;

- If you take an AP class, take the AP test. The test score does not count towards your GPA;

- There is a grade advantage in doing well in an AP class. Many students ask, "Is a B in an AP class better than an A in a regular class?" Below is a table on calculating GPA with and without an AP class (using AP English and Regular English as an example):

Comparing AP and Regular class grading for GPA							
With AP English				With regular English			
AP English	A	5	AP English	B	4	English	A	4	English	B	3
History	A	4	History	A	4	History	A	4	History	A	4
Math	A	4	Math	A	4	Math	A	4	Math	A	4
Science	A	4	Science	A	4	Science	A	4	Science	A	4
		17			16			16			15
		4.25			4			4			3.75
Key - Regular AP number/letter grading - A(5), B(4), C(3), D(2)							
Key - Regular class number/letter grading - A(4), B(3), C(2), D(1)							
Calculation: Assign number to the letter grade, add numbers, divide total by number of classes							

AP English with a B yields the same GPA as regular English with an A. Because colleges want to see students who have challenged themselves throughout high school and have taken the most challenging versions of classes available to them, the B in an AP class over an A in a regular class produces the same GPA and is potentially more attractive to college admissions officers.

Honors Courses
The term 'Honors' course is a common label applied to courses, predominantly at the high school level, that are considered to be more academically challenging and prestigious. There are no specific standards or universal definition for Honors courses and, consequently, they may vary greatly in design, content, quality, or academic challenge from school to school, and even from course to course within a school. Students enrolled in Honors courses generally receive greater academic recognition and possibly, if the course awards weighted grades, a numerical advantage when it comes to grading.

Historically, Honors courses entailed more demanding college preparatory coursework and were intended for the highest achieving or most academically accelerated students in a school. In many cases, students need to meet certain prerequisites to be admitted to an honors course, such as a teacher recommendation or an average grade of B or higher in a previous course. Honors courses may be the highest-level courses or "track" offered by the school, or they may be above "college prep," but below specialized courses such as Advanced Placement or International Baccalaureate. In some schools, however, Advanced Placement and International Baccalaureate courses will be considered the school's Honors courses.

Advanced College Project (ACP) courses
Advance College Project (ACP) is a dual-enrollment partnership between Indiana University (IU) and select high schools throughout Indiana and surrounding states. IU courses taught through the ACP program provide both high school and college credits (known as concurrent or dual enrollment) and allow students to fulfill high school graduation requirements as well as start building their college career. As with honors

ACADEMIC PREPARATION

classes, additional credit can be earned for these classes, which will affect a student's GPA. Colleges will typically have an evaluation structure for each of these types of advanced course and classes.

International Baccalaureate (IB)
International Baccalaureate students complete a range of subjects at a high level and, with a good score, are viewed by admissions officers as having challenged themselves in high school. Credit can be given dependent on scores and subjects.

Dual Enrollment /Credit Courses
Many high schools are now partnering with local colleges to provide dual enrollment courses. In these programs, students can earn college credit by taking the same courses as students at a nearby college. Some dual enrollment classes take place in high school during the school day, whilst others require students to attend classes on college campus. Because of the variety of dual enrollment options, colleges do not have a fixed policy on using these classes for credit. However, having dual enrollment courses on your application is certainly an indication to admissions officers that you have challenged yourself academically.

2.2 STANDARDIZED TESTS

If you are applying to college, it is very likely that you will be required to take one or more standardized tests. The two standardized tests that are most widely used for college admissions purposes are: the SAT (Scholastic Aptitude Test) and the ACT (American College Testing). Both tests are accepted by US colleges and are used by admissions officers as an indication of a student's academic ability. Both tests are designed to demonstrate college readiness, but the tests vary in content matter, structure, timing, and scoring. It is valuable to understand the differences in order to make a decision about which test might be best for you. Ideally, you should take both tests (preferably in practice form) and then choose the one that suits you best.

2.2.1 The SAT

The SAT assesses students in two subject areas: Evidence-Based Reading & Writing (EBRW) and Math (M). There is also an optional essay. The SAT is divided into sections as follows:

Evidence-Based Reading & Writing (EBRW) Sections
        Reading Test - 52 questions/65 minutes
        Writing and Language Test - 44 questions/35 minutes
Math (M) Sections
        Math Test - No Calculator (Multiple choice + student produced response): 20 questions/25 minutes
        Math Test - Calculator permitted (Multiple choice + student produced response): 38 questions/55 minutes
Optional Essay Section
        1 prompt/50 minutes

The required sections of the SAT take 3 hours to complete. The optional writing component (the essay) adds 50 minutes to the test, making the full test 3 hours and 50 minutes. The key concepts tested on each section of the SAT are:

Reading Test
   Command of Evidence, Words in Context, and Analysis of Social Studies/Science.
Writing and Language Test
   Same as Reading Test + Expression of Ideas and Standard English Conventions.
Math Test
   No Calculator (Multiple choice + student produced response): Linear equations and systems, Quantitative skills, and some Geometry and Trigonometry.
Math Test
   Calculator permitted (Multiple choice + student produced response): Same as first Math test + manipulation of complex equations.
Optional Essay
   Proof of focus, organization, and precision in writing and analysis.

2.2.2   The ACT

The ACT tests students in **English** (E), **Math** (M), **Reading** (R), and **Science** (S). There is an optional essay. The ACT is divided into sections as follows:

   English: 75 questions/45 minutes
   Mathematics: 60 questions/60 minutes
   Reading: 40 questions/35 minutes
   Science: 40 questions/35 minutes
   Optional Writing (Essay): 1 essay prompt/40 minutes

The required sections of the ACT take 2 hours and 55 minutes. The optional writing component (the essay) adds 40 extra minutes to the test, making the full test 3 hours and 35 minutes. The key concepts tested on each section of the ACT are as follows:

English
   Usage/Mechanics and Rhetorical Skills
Mathematics
   Pre-Algebra and Elementary Algebra, Intermediate Algebra and Coordinate Geometry, and Plane Geometry and Trigonometry
Reading
   Arts and Literature and Social Studies and Sciences
Science
   Data representations, research summaries, and conflicting viewpoints
Optional Writing
   Ideas and analysis, development and support, organization, and language use and conventions.

2.2.3   SCORING THE SAT AND ACT

The two tests differ in scoring in a significant way through the reporting of scaled points. Simply put, the SAT inflates scores and the ACT deflates scores.

ACADEMIC PREPARATION

SAT SCORING
The composite score range on the SAT is 400-1600. The lowest score you can earn on each of the three sections of the SAT is 200. So, if you answered no questions right and many questions wrong, you would get 200. Thus, the lowest potential combined score one can get on the two main sections (EBRW and M) of the SAT is 400. Alternatively, if you get every SAT question right (or nearly every question right on some test administration dates), the most you can score is 800 on each section (EBRW and M). Thus, the highest combined score one can earn on the SAT is 1600. The average scores for Americans taking the test come in at just above or below 500 per section depending on the year or exact test date of administration.

Scoring the SAT Essay
The SAT essay is marked by two readers, each awarding a score between 1 and 4 for three distinct domains:
- Reading
- Analysis
- Writing

The two scores on each of the three domains are added together to give an individual score ranging from 2 to 8 and a cumulative score ranging from 6 to 24. This score is not scaled and you will be given the raw score. It is not included in the overall composite score. For more detailed information on SAT scoring, look at: https://collegereadiness.collegeboard.org/sat/scores/understanding-scores/essay

ACT SCORING
Scoring on the ACT looks completely different, firstly because it has more sections than the SAT, and secondly because it calculates your average score on all the sections that make up the test. This score is referred to as your composite score. The highest composite score one can earn on the ACT is 36, and the lowest is 1. So, for example, the student who gets 30 on the ACT (well done!) may have scored on each section like this:

- 33 on the English section
- 29 on the Math section
- 31 on the Reading section
- 28 on the Science section

Averaged out, the calculation is 33+29+31+28 = 121/4 = 30.25. ACT rounds to .50, so this score is rounded down to 30. If a score of 30.75, it would be rounded up to 31.

Scoring the ACT Essay
The ACT has two readers review your essay, and each reader gives your essay a score between 1 and 6 for four distinct domains:

- Ideas and Analysis
- Development and Support
- Organization
- Language Use and Conventions

The raw Writing (essay) score on the ACT is the sum of these scores (up to a maximum raw score of 48). The ACT then scales your score according to its standard 36-point scale.

GETTING THROUGH IT TOGETHER

SAT - ACT Comparison		
	SAT	**ACT**
Time	3 hours Optional 50-minute essay Total of 3 hours 50 minutes	2 hours 55 minutes Optional 40 minute writing test Total of 3 hours 25 minutes
No. of questions	154 questions 1 min 10 seconds per question	215 questions 49 seconds per question
Content and Time/question ratio	Reading: 52 questions/65 minutes Writing & Language: 44 questions/35 minutes Math No Calculator: 20 questions/25 minutes Math with Calculator: 38 questions/55 minutes Optional Essay: 1 essay prompt/50 minutes	Reading: 40 questions/35 minutes English: 75 questions/45 minutes Math: 60 questions/60 minutes Science: 40 questions/35 minutes Optional Essay: 1 essay prompt/40 minutes
Time per question	Reading: 1 minute 15 seconds Writing & Language: 47 seconds Math No Calculator: 1 minutes 15 seconds Math with Calculator: 1 minute 26 seconds	Reading: 52 seconds English: 36 seconds Math: 1 minute Science: 52 seconds
Scoring	Score range 400-1600 based on 2 sections at 800 each: Evidence-Based Reading & Writing (EBRW) and Math Essay scored separately	Score range 1-36 across the test Raw scores for 4 subsections converted to scaled scores Essay scored separately
Key Concepts: English - Writing, & Language	EBRW - Standard English conventions Analysis and expression of ideas Words in Context Command of evidence	Grammar Punctuation Rhetorical Skills Sentence Structure
Key Concepts: Reading	EBRW – Literary passage Science passage with chart or graph Global theme or founding documents passage	Prose fiction Social studies passage Humanities passage Natural Sciences passage
Key Concepts: Mathematics	Algebra, geometry, statistics analysis, linear equations, trigonometry. Also some charts and graphs.	Algebra I and II, geometry, some trigonometry
Key Concepts: Science	No Science section on the SAT	Science-based passages with graphs, charts, tables, and research summaries
Key Concepts: Essay	Proof of focus Organization Precision in writing & analysis Analysis of argument and theme	Ideas and Analysis Development and Support Organization Language Use and Conventions
Cost	Test only $47.50 With essay $64.50	Test only $50.50 With essay $67
	Additional fees may apply for late registration Fee waivers possible	

ACADEMIC PREPARATION

2.2.4 SUPER SCORING

Super scoring is a process whereby colleges take the best scores from each section of a particular test from multiple sittings. For example: If you take the SAT twice, and the first time you got a 650 on the SAT Math and 720 on the SAT Evidence-Based Reading and Writing (EBRW), and the second time you got a 680 on Math and 690 on EBRW, colleges that super score will use the 720 EBRW score and the 680 Math score to create a new higher score.

SAT SUPER SCORING

Colleges know that many students take the SAT at least twice in preparation for college applications. While most students will score within the same range overall, they often have one section score that goes up the second time around and that increase indicates to the officers that the student has the capacity to engage with the material at a deep level and work hard. Super scoring also helps colleges maintain a level of prestige. By super scoring, colleges are able to report higher test score averages overall across all of the admitted students, the results of which indicate the level of competitiveness for places at that college.

If a college does not super score, it will generally take the highest composite score from a single test sitting if it receives multiple score reports for the same student. For example, if a student takes the test twice and gets a 700 Math score and 640 EBRW score on the first one, and a 730 Math score and 630 EBRW score on the second test, the college will take the score from the second sitting because the total score is higher (1340 from the first sitting and 1360 from the second). For the student who has pretty consistent scores, super scoring may not make too much of a difference. But, for the student who has an effective study plan, it can dramatically improve the composite score. This is especially true if the first scores were lopsided, where one score was much higher than the other. In the example below, it can be seen how raising a score in one section can make a significant impact on the composite score. With effort, and targeted study on EBRW, the score was raised from 600 to 700. But, on that same sitting, the Math score slipped to 720. The highest single composite score (from the 2nd sitting) is 1420, but with super scoring, it would be 1500:

First sitting	EBRW 600
	Math 800
	Composite 1400
Second sitting	EBRW 700
	Math 720
	Composite 1420
Super score	EBRW 700 (from 2nd sitting)
	Math 800 (from 1st sitting)
	Composite 1500

It also matters if you plan on applying to colleges early and want to avoid being deferred. Quite often a student is deferred because he or she is a borderline applicant. Having a stronger test score can edge you towards being a stronger applicant.

ACT SUPER SCORING

Each section of the ACT is given a scaled score between 1 and 36. These area scores are then averaged together to get your composite score, which also ranges between 1 and 36. If a college super scores the ACT, it will take your highest Math, Science, Reading, and English scores that you achieved on any of the dates you took the test. Then, it will average these together for a new composite so that you'll end up with your highest possible composite score.

While super scoring means that you can take chances by sitting the test, effectively, as many times as you wish to get the scores you want, beware of taking it too many times. Colleges can request reporting of all ACT sittings and if a student has taken the ACT more than, say, three of four time times with inconsistent scores, they may view the applicant less favorably. That said, as long as you don't go overboard, taking the ACT more than once can work very well in an applicant's favor if you're applying to schools that super score.

2.2.5 WHEN TO TAKE THE TESTS

Take a practice ACT as soon after the PSAT as you can. Then, you will be able to compare the two. If you like the ACT, take the first official test in December or February. You then have three or four more chances before summer to take additional tests if you need to. If you prefer the SAT, take the official test as soon after the PSAT as you can and, preferably before winter break. You then have several opportunities to take more tests before summer. Remember to factor in your SAT subject test dates too, and keep in mind:

- College Board does not offer SAT Subject tests in March;
- You cannot take the SAT and SAT subject tests on the same day;
- You can take three SAT subject tests on one day (unless you are taking a foreign language with listening test, in which case you can only take one).

ACT or SAT? – WHICH TEST IS BEST FOR YOU?
The only way to know which is the best test for you is, of course, to try both. Practice tests are often available at a community level at local schools and libraries, and at a commercial level through private tutoring organizations. When you have taken both, you can then decide on which you want to concentrate. There are three questions to consider when deciding on the best test for you:

- **Which of the tests do you like more?**
  This is not a trick question! There are many questions to ask yourself within this larger question, such as: How do the tests FEEL to you? Which format do you prefer? Do you like having the Science component? Which style of question do you prefer? How did you find the timing?

- **How well did you do on the Science component of the ACT?**
  Only the ACT has a Science component and, if you are good at Science (or, more specifically, interpreting scientific data, since that is how many of the Science questions are structured) consider how a good score on Science adds to your composite score.

- **On which of the tests did you get the highest score?**
  Take a look at the Score equivalents table below. It might be glaringly obvious to which test you are better suited but, sometimes, the results are too similar. If this is the case, go with your gut feel and go back to question 1 – which of the tests do you LIKE more?

ACADEMIC PREPARATION

SAT and ACT Scoring Equivalents Table

SAT SCORE	ACT EQUIVALENT	SAT SCORE	ACT EQUIVALENT
1600-1570	36	1120-1100	22
1560-1530	35	1090-1060	21
1520-1490	34	1050-1030	20
1480-1450	33	1020-990	19
1440-1420	32	980-960	18
1410-1390	31	950-920	17
1380-1360	30	910-880	16
1350-1330	29	870-830	15
1320-1300	28	820-780	14
1290-1260	27	770-730	13
1250-1230	26	720-690	12
1220-1200	25	680-650	11
1190-1160	24	640-620	10
1150-1130	23	610-590	9

2.2.6 THE SAT SUBJECT TESTS

SAT Subject tests are useful for the student who wants to show competence in specific subject areas. It is always a good idea to take a practice test before going into the real thing. Few schools require these tests for evaluation for admission. However, over the past few years, it has become apparent that many more schools 'recommend' them or will 'consider' them if submitted, especially if they are related to a declared major or 'statement of interest' in a major.

To be a competitive candidate for admission to most Ivy League and Ivy League-level colleges, plan on taking two or three SAT Subject Tests at the end of the academic year in which you have taken a rigorous course. For example, if you take Chemistry in sophomore year, did well in the class, but do not intend to continue to AP level, you should consider taking the Chemistry SAT Subject test. You can study for it alongside your regular study for class finals and, if you do well, it is a nice addition to your résumé. For these types of schools, and if you are planning to take Math, you will need to take Math Level 2.

SAT Subject tests:

- Are based on material that is taught in a regular high school class;
- Are scored on a scale ranging from 200 to 800;
- Are one hour long (except for the foreign language with listening tests);
- Are not offered on all SAT test dates. For example, the Italian test is only available once a year in June and the Chinese test is only available once a year, in November. Check for dates on the College Board website when you plan your testing schedule;
- Apart from language with listening, three tests can be taken on one day;
- You can apply to take one test and on test day, if you decide you want to try others, just stay and take them. You will be billed later.

SAT Subject tests are available in the following subjects:

Math	Math Level 1
	Math Level 2
Science	Biology (Choice of Ecological or Molecular Biology)
	Chemistry
	Physics
English	English Literature
History	U.S. History
	World History
Languages	Spanish
	Spanish with Listening
	French
	French with Listening
	Chinese with Listening
	Italian
	German
	German with Listening
	Modern Hebrew
	Latin
	Japanese with Listening
	Korean with Listening

If you are a good student, the SAT subject tests are a way to show off your competence. Take at least two and submit the scores if they are over 550 for less competitive schools and over 650 for more competitive schools. Make sure you do a few practice tests in your chosen subjects. The structure may be different than in tests you take in class. But, remember, it is content based and, as such, you either know the content or you don't. You don't want to be taking these tests over and over again. When thinking about the SAT Subject tests, consider the following:

Why You Should Consider Taking SAT Subject Tests

The SAT Subject Tests are one-hour-long exams that give you the opportunity to demonstrate knowledge and showcase achievement in specific subjects. They provide a fair and reliable measure of your achievement in high school—information that can help enhance your college application portfolio. SAT Subject Tests measure how well you know a particular subject area and your ability to apply that knowledge. SAT Subject Tests aren't connected to specific textbooks or teaching methods. The content of each test evolves to reflect the latest trends in what is taught in typical high school courses in the corresponding subject.

How Colleges Use SAT Subject Test Scores

Colleges use SAT Subject Test scores to gain insight into your academic background and achievement in specific subject areas. They can use this information, in combination with other factors (high school

ACADEMIC PREPARATION

grades, letters of recommendation, extracurricular activities, essays, etc.), to make admission or placement decisions. Even schools that don't require the tests often review them during the application process because the scores can give a fuller picture of your academic achievements. Many colleges also use Subject Tests for course placement and advising and some schools allow you to place out of introductory courses with good grades in certain SAT Subject Tests.

Deciding on what SAT Subject Tests to Take

SAT Subject Tests are the only college admission tests where you can choose the subjects in which you are tested. You select the Subject Test(s) and can take up to three tests in one sitting. With the exception of listening tests, you can even decide to change the subject or number of tests you want to take on the day of the test.

The SAT Subject Tests that you take should be based on the subject areas you enjoy in school as well as your academic strengths. The tests are a great way to indicate interest in specific majors or programs of study (e.g., Engineering, Premed, Cultural Studies). Certain colleges or programs of study require or recommend specific tests, such as Math or Science, so it's important to make sure you understand the policies prior to choosing which Subject Tests to take. If you have questions or concerns about admission policies, contact admission officers at individual schools.

When to Take SAT Subject Tests

Check the recommended preparation guidelines for each Subject Test at SATSubjectTests.org (click on each subject to view) to make sure you've completed the recommended course work. In general, you'll want to take SAT Subject Tests right after you've completed the recommended classes, even in your first or second years of high school, because the material will still be fresh in your mind. For language tests, however, you should not consider testing until after you've studied the language for at least two years. Check online to see when the Subject Tests in which you are interested are offered. You should also think about college application deadlines. Go to bigfuture.org to look up policies for specific colleges.
For full details of contents of each test, go to: https://collegereadiness.collegeboard.org/pdf/sat-subject-tests-student-guide.pdf. SAT Subject Test preparation books are often available in school and local libraries and for sale on Amazon. There are official study preparation books for each subject published by College Board and numerous other books published by companies, such as Barron's and Princeton Review.

2.2.7 TEST OPTIONAL

There are many schools that do not use standardized tests as part of their admission evaluation procedure. If considering not taking a test, you should definitely confirm your status as an applicant on the following points before proceeding:

- Are tests required for placement purposes?
- Does not having test scores eliminate you from consideration for any merit scholarships?

FairTest.org lists over 800 'test optional' colleges, not all of which are four-year institutions. You must pay attention to the small print within each listing as colleges may have restrictions on the policy.

2.3 PREPARING A RÉSUMÉ

A résumé is a place to show off your hard work. It can speak volumes for you, especially when you cannot present yourself in person. You can use your résumé to apply for letters of recommendation, jobs, internships, and scholarship applications. Many colleges now also give the option to download a résumé with your college application and you should take advantage of this additional opportunity to showcase yourself. Make sure to keep it updated with information on all new activities and qualifications.

You should aim to keep your résumé to one page only. The reader will lose interest after any more. So, the key is to keep it concise. A well-prepared résumé is useful for several reasons:

- It helps you keep track of your accomplishments. When the time comes to complete college applications, it is easy to forget a few things. A résumé will help remind you of every pertinent detail;
- A résumé gives college admissions officers a snapshot of all they need to know about a student - not all colleges offer facilities to download the résumé, but many do and, when given the opportunity, it is wise to submit it;
- It can spark a college essay. Reflecting on experiences from summer jobs, volunteer work, or school activities may lead to a unique essay topic that will make you stand out;
- Activities and achievements can lead to scholarships. Scholarship committees look for participation in extracurricular activities. Some activities are particularly desirable to some colleges. Activities as diverse as scouting, marching band, and scuba diving, for example, will give you a potential edge over students who do more usual types of activities. Such diverse activities may also open you up to finding good scholarship opportunities;
- An impressive résumé can lead to summer internships, jobs, or study-abroad opportunities that subsequently will strengthen your college applications;
- Having a résumé at hand when requesting letters of recommendation is very useful. Teachers and counselors may only know the student from their accomplishments in a subject or within the academic environment. With a résumé, they can see that you are more than the person they know from only the classroom;
- When attending college fairs, college visits to your school, or even touring colleges, you may have the opportunity to hand over your résumé, which will make you memorable as being well organized and mature;
- College life is full of opportunities, in and out of the classroom, and the choices can be overwhelming. Listing activities and accomplishments can help you figure out what you want to continue doing and that will help you in your research to find colleges that offer the greatest opportunities.

A note about the spelling of the word résumé: technically, it should be résumé with the accents on é. However, when submitting online, there is the danger that some systems may substitute those accented letters with strange characters. It is therefore safer to NOT use the accented é if you're submitting online. If you are sending a hard copy, however, I suggest using the correct spelling with the accents on the two é.

The best time to start building your résumé is during sophomore year because:

- It can help you identify the academic areas you need to work on. An early résumé will give you an idea of what needs attention before it's too late. It will also get you thinking about the importance of high SAT and ACT scores;

ACADEMIC PREPARATION

- It can help you target non-academic areas that you need to improve upon. Once you see gaps in your experiences, you still have plenty of time to get involved in something new before application time;
- A résumé is a great introduction to a college recruiter. It is not always possible to have long talks with college recruiters at college fairs, so a quick introduction and passing on your résumé will give you the chance to connect with as many recruiters as possible;
- As you write your résumé, you will be reminded of people who may be willing to give you a reference. College applications ask for letters of recommendation from teachers and counselors, and sometimes from coaches, mentors, and employers. This is a great time to start lining up your options now.

Remember...
- A poorly written résumé can be worse than no résumé at all. Please proofread carefully to ensure correct spelling (don't rely only on spellcheck), grammar, and punctuation;
- The résumé should be in a professional-looking and easy-to-read font, such as Times New Roman, Arial, or Calibri. The formatting should catch the eye of the recipient and bring attention to key items;
- Be honest. When students lie—or even stretch the truth—on their résumés, they can be found out, which causes embarrassment at best and withdrawal of offers at worst. Ensure that all information is accurate.

It will help if you start by listing all your achievements throughout your high school years in a simple format. Use the template below to organize your thoughts (and jog your memory!) You might want to ask your parents if they can think of anything too. It amazes me how students forget that there were on Honor Roll for the past two years, or that they organized a fundraising activity for the French club. Those are things that need to go on your résumé.

You may find that there will be some overlap of activities. For example, you were captain of the lacrosse team, which spans both the 'Sports' and 'Leadership' categories. You will not need to list them separately, so just consider which is the most suitable category for your purposes. If you plan to continue playing lacrosse, or are applying for a scholarship for lacrosse, for example, then you should put your captainship of the lacrosse team under the 'Sports' category. Examples of the categories and what to include in each of them are:

Academic Achievements

- Honor Roll (years achieved)
- GATE (Gifted and Talented Education) Student
- GPA
- Advanced Placement Classes
- College Courses
- Certificates, Passes, Grades for extracurricular summer/online courses

Awards, Nominations, Recognitions, Citations, Special Projects

- Prizes, Recognition, Certificates – Foreign language, Science, Math, etc.
- Music awards (e.g. Grade certification for piano, flute, etc.)
- Institutional awards (e.g. Eagle Scout, Community Service Award)

GETTING THROUGH IT TOGETHER

- Arts awards (Art, Drama, Dance, Speech, etc.)
- School recognition awards (Valedictorian, School representative/ambassador, etc.)

Extracurricular Activities

- Membership to Academic clubs (e.g. Junior United Nations, Italian Club)
- Membership to Institutional clubs/societies (e.g. Scouts, Girl Guides, Lions Club)
- Church activities (e.g. Choir, family dinner, Sunday school)
- Music, theater, and drama (indicate any leadership roles and leading dramatic/singing roles)
- School activities (leadership, year book, journalism, photography, broadcasting)

Sports

For each sport, list important positions. For example:

- Leadership and/or coaching roles
- High school team – JV, Varsity, winning tournaments/awards
- Club team – winning tournaments, awards

Volunteer/Community Service

List the activities in which you were involved in and out of school. Indicate those activities in which you participate on an ongoing basis. For example:

- Reading tutor (6 – 8 year olds) (2 hour/week, 20**-present)
- Spanish Immersion School, San Diego (2 hours/week, 20**-present)

Competitions/Fairs

Individual or team participation in Science fairs, Robotics fairs, Poetry slams, Screen-writing competitions, etc. List the activity and your contribution. For example:

- Co-designer, Solar Racing Car Project, San Diego Science Fair, March 20** (2nd place)

Work Experience/Internships

List all jobs – paid and unpaid – that you have done. For example:

- Part-time sales assistant, A store, San Francisco (8 hours/week, 7 months, 20**)
- Waiter, Top Restaurant, San Francisco (10 hours/week, 2 months, Summer, 201**)
- Babysitter for two families (approx. 20 hours/month, 5 years, 20** to 20**)
- Intern, ABC Boutique, San Francisco – shadowed Senior Buyer (5 weeks, Summer 20**)

Summer Experiences

List summer programs taken within your high school years (including summer pre high school). For example:

- Summer camps (sports, church, etc. – include leadership/counseling roles)
- Academic programs – domestic and overseas, foreign language programs
- Athletic programs – sport, level, leadership positions
- Music programs – e.g., band camp

ACADEMIC PREPARATION

- Community and outreach programs – domestic and overseas, activity, responsibilities, leadership.

Tutoring/Mentoring Roles (if not indicated in another category)

- Academic - Teacher's aides, after-school tutoring, help in special education programs, homework/reading helper, etc. (indicate length of time you have participated in each activity)
- Extracurricular – Horseback-riding, Special Olympics, piano teacher, etc. (include length of time you have participated in each activity
- Peer tutor (include subject(s) you tutor, time per week, and length of time)
- Homework helper (include age of children you help, subject(s), and times per week)

Leadership Positions (if not indicated in another category)

- Member/leader of freshmen orientation program (include dates)
- Student representative on school and/or parent group committees (include dates)
- Member/leader of fundraising activities (include dates)

Languages

If you speak more than one language make sure you put this in your résumé, especially if you are interested in studying language(s), global politics, and/or international relations. You can even indicate your level of proficiency in each of your languages if you wish. For example:

- English (fluent), Spanish (fluent), French (good), Mandarin (beginner)

Other Skills

If you have skills that are reflective of your particular interests (and especially if they relate to your chosen major or statement of interest), you could add them here. For example:

- Computer skills (Python, C++)

When you have completed your tables, it's time to build your résumé, using all the relevant information. This takes some concentration to get it right, but once it's done, it's done and you will have a very valuable document on hand. You should aim to keep your résumé to one page in length. If you have done nothing within a certain category, omit the heading and work with what you have.

Achievements Template (Use one for each grade of High School)

Academic Awards/Honors	
Other Awards	
Extracurricular Activities	
Sports	
Volunteer/ Community Service	
Competitions/ Fairs	
Work Experience/Internships	
Summer Experiences	
Tutoring /Mentoring Roles	
Leadership Positions	
Languages	
Special Skills	

ACADEMIC PREPARATION

Sample Format and information for your Résumé

PERSONAL INFORMATION
    Name and Address
    Phone Number and E-mail address

ACADEMIC INFORMATION
    Name of high school
    GPA / Honor Roll
    AP Classes and test scores, SAT, ACT, and SAT Subject test scores, etc.
    College/online classes
    Awards, nominations, recognitions, citations, special projects

EXTRACURRICULAR ACTIVITIES, CLUBS, SOCIETIES
    School, Community, Church

LEADERSHIP ROLES
    Holding office in class, sports, clubs
    Taking initiative or responsibility for projects
    Leadership camp participation

WORK
    Work experience, Internships, and Leadership positions
    Tutoring or mentorship roles

WORKSHOPS/SUMMER PROGRAMS
    Camps, programs, seminars, projects, special classes, competitions

SPORTS
    Participation and achievements

COMMUNITY/VOLUNTEER WORK
    Part-time and On-going

SPECIAL INTERESTS
    Hobbies, Musical instrument/band, choir, painting, photography, robotics, etc.

LANGUAGES
    Indicate level of proficiency (Fluent, Advanced, Intermediate, Beginner, if appropriate)

SPECIAL SKILLS
    Organizational, Computer programming, Public speaking.

*****

DAVID SMITH

ADDRESS: 222 Jefferson Avenue
City, CA 94010

EMAIL: davidnasmith@gmail.com
TEL: (200) 222-2222

EDUCATION: Jefferson High School, Class of 20**

ACADEMIC ACHIEVEMENTS:
- Honor Roll (Grades 9-11)
- ACT - 28
- APs - US History (Grade 4), Italian (Grade 4), English Language and Composition (3)
- APs (Senior year) – English Literature US Government & Politics
- SAT Subject Tests - US History (620), Spanish (600), Math Level II (580)

AWARDS, NOMINATIONS, RECOGNITIONS, CITATIONS, SPECIAL PROJECTS

20**   Most Improved Player, Golf
20**   ABC Summer Program – Certificates: Creative Writing, Journalism, Architecture
20**   DEF Summer Language Program – Certificate, Advanced Spanish

TUTORING/MENTORING ROLES (2011-2015)
- Summer camp soccer coach, Sports Facility, CA
- Soccer Referee, Jefferson Soccer Camp, CA
- Camp Counselor (4 years)
- Spanish Homework Tutor (1 year)

COMMUNITY SERVICE:
- Counselor, Jefferson Spanish Immersion Pre-School (1 year, 20**))
- Coordinator, Buddies program, Jefferson Assisted Living Center (2 years, 20**-present)

SPORTS:
- Golf: Captain, Varsity Golf Team, Jefferson High School (20**)
- Track
- Soccer

WORK EXPERIENCE/INTERNSHIPS:
- Front desk Reception, Jefferson Recreation Center (3 months, 20**)
- Children's Party Host, Jefferson Soccer Camp (2 months, 20**)
- Sales Assistant, Jefferson Athletic Clothing Sore, (3 months, 20**)

ACTIVITIES AND INTERESTS: Travel, Languages, Journalism, Art, Golf

LANGUAGES: English (fluent), Spanish (Very good)

****

ACADEMIC PREPARATION

2.4 LETTERS OF RECOMMENDATION

Generally, all selective colleges and universities require letters of recommendation with your application, usually one from your guidance counselor and at least one from a teacher. Letters of recommendation are typically submitted electronically through the school specific- supplements on the Common Application. Points to remember when asking for letters of recommendation include:

When asking a Teacher:

- Choose a teacher with whom you have a good relationship and/or in whose class you did well;
- Choose a teacher from a core class subject, e.g., English, Math, or Science;
- A teacher from junior year is best, preferably no teacher from below sophomore year;
- Most teachers will only know you in the context of your activities in their class. In order for them to 'know' you better and get a picture of you as a whole person, give them a copy of your résumé;
- Some teachers might ask to see your most recent transcript, so have a copy ready when you speak to them about your letter.

When asking a Counselor:

- If you don't have a relationship with your school counselor, make an appointment to see him or her;
- Take a copy of your transcript – it is available online, but it makes you look organized and efficient);
- Take a copy of your list of colleges to which you wish to apply and ask their opinion;
- Give them a copy of your résumé.

When they agree, make sure that you do the following:

- Tell them how much you appreciate their writing a letter for you;
- Keep them informed of deadlines and send email reminders a week in advance;
- Send a 'Thank you' email or hand-written note.

NOTE: On the applications, make sure you tick the box to waive your rights to see the letters of recommendation. Colleges can get suspicious if they see that you want to see your letters before they do.

Letters of recommendation are not necessarily actual letters, but can be an evaluation sheet on which the counselor or teacher assigns a level of competency for a variety of personal qualities. The table below is a sample rubric of the criteria teachers and counselors may use when assessing a student and writing a letter of recommendation:

Sample – Counselor/Teacher Student Evaluation Rubric								
No Basis		Below Average	Average	Good (above average)	Very Good (well above average)	Excellent (top 10%)	Outstanding (top 5%)	Top Few
	Academic Achievement							
	Intellectual Promise							
	Quality of Writing							
	Creative Thought							
	Productive Discussion							
	Faculty Respect							
	Disciplined Habits							
	Maturity							
	Motivation							
	Leadership							
	Integrity							
	Reaction to Setbacks							
	Concern for Others							
	Self-confidence							
	Initiative							
	OVERALL							

The harder you work, the luckier you get.

- Gary Player

ACADEMIC PREPARATION

2.5 PARENT POINTER – HOW TO HELP IN THE ACADEMIC STAGE

Sophomore and Junior years can be challenging, but for the student concentrating on getting into a 'good college,' the concern about managing the workload and getting good grades, coupled with the possible attendant fear of failure, can be sources of anxiety. Strategies to help them during this stage include:

Listen to your teen's concerns and issues
Try not to 'fix' things for them but give them suggestions on how they can help themselves.

Try not to insist on their finding a "passion"
Show interest and respect for their creativity, but try not to make it more than it is.

Help them build self-esteem and confidence with appropriate praise
Ensure that the praise is directed at their accomplishment, rather than your feelings about it.
For example, saying, "Congratulations on acing your history test – that must feel so good after all that hard work you put in," is a better way to help your teen feel good about themselves than saying, "I am so proud of you for acing the history test – I knew you could do it."

Help them with studying
Some students benefit more than others from having someone help them with their studies. You may be able to help by offering, for example, to ask practice questions when they are studying for a chemistry test or history pop quiz. You can also offer to listen to presentations or essays.

To be in your children's memories tomorrow, you have to be in their lives today.

— Unknown

CHAPTER 3
CHOOSING COLLEGES

Two roads diverged in a wood and I, I took the road less traveled.

- Robert Frost

CHOOSING COLLEGES

3.1 GETTING STARTED ON THE COLLEGE LIST

In the United States, there are over 2,000 accredited four-year higher education institutions, all of which have been categorized according to their admissions statistics. A college's admissions statistic is a factor that indicates its level of selectivity. Colleges are ranked according to this and other statistics into categories, referred to here as: Most Selective, Highly Selective, Selective, and Moderately Selective. The categories can generally be divided into criteria by admittance percentage and ACT and SAT scores.

An admittance percentage is generally calculated by taking the number of students accepted into a freshman class from the number of applicants. This is not the number of applicants that actually accepted and entered – only the number that the college admissions officers accepted from the pool of applicants. A college with a 5% admittance rate reflects the reality that it accepted only 2,188 applicants from a pool of 43,997, thus making this particular school one of the most competitive schools in the country, and placing it in the "Most Selective" category. Conversely, a college with an admittance rate of 78% (with 14,029 students accepted from an applicant pool of 17,918 in this case) indicates that this is a significantly less competitive school and therefore is in the "Moderately Selective" category.

Examples of colleges within each category are in the tables below. It is worth noting that requirements and grade ranges change with each applications cycle. It is therefore advisable to check on that information when you are choosing colleges.

Examples of Colleges in the MOST SELECTIVE category	
Accept fewer than 20% of all applicants, Average combined SAT (CR & M) 1300+, Average composite ACT 29+	
Amherst College	Northwestern University
Bowdoin College	Pomona College
Brown University	Princeton University
California Institute of Technology	Rice University
Claremont McKenna College	Stanford University
Columbia University	Swarthmore College
Cornell University	Tufts University
Dartmouth University	United States Air Force Academy
Duke University	University of Chicago
Georgetown University	University of Pennsylvania
Harvard University	Vanderbilt University
Harvey Mudd College	Washington University
Johns Hopkins University	Washington and Lee University
Massachusetts Institute of Technology	Williams College
Middlebury College	

Examples of colleges in the HIGHLY SELECTIVE category	

Accept fewer than 40% of all applicants, Average combined SAT (CR + M) 1260+, Average composite ACT 28+	
Barnard College	Macalester College
Bates College	New York University
Boston College	Northeastern University
Brandeis University	Oberlin College
Bucknell University	Scripps College
Carleton College	Tulane University
Carnegie Mellon University	United States Military Academy
Colby College	United States Naval Academy
Colgate University	University of California, Berkeley
College of William and Mary	University of California, Los Angeles
College of the Holy Cross	University of Michigan, Ann Arbor
Connecticut College	University of North Carolina at Chapel Hill
Cooper Union	University of Notre Dame
Davidson College	University of Richmond
Emory University	University of Rochester
Franklin and Marshall College	University of Southern California
Georgia Institute of Technology	University of Virginia
Hamilton College	Vassar College
Haverford College	Wake Forest University
Kenyon College	Wellesley College
Lehigh University	Wesleyan University

CHOOSING COLLEGES

Examples of colleges in the VERY SELECTIVE category		
Accept fewer than 60% of all applicants, Average combined SAT (CR + M) 1190+, Average composite ACT 26+		
American University		Pitzer College
Babson College		Rensselaer Polytechnic Institute
Bard College		Rhodes College
Bentley University		State U New York at Geneseo
Boston University		State U New York at Binghamton
Brigham Young University		Santa Clara University
Bryn Mawr College		Shimer College
Case Western Reserve University		Skidmore College
Clemson University		Smith College
Colorado School of Mines		Southern Methodist University
Denison University		St. Olaf College
Dickinson College		Stevens Institute of Technology
Emerson College		Stony Brook University
Fordham University		Union College
George Washington University		University of Florida
Gettysburg College		University of Georgia
Hobart and William Smith Colleges		University of Maryland, College Park
Lafayette College		University of Miami
Marist College		University of Minnesota, Twin Cities
Mount Holyoke College		University of Pittsburgh
Occidental College		Villanova University
Ohio State University		Whitman College
Reed College		Worcester Polytechnic Institute

Examples of colleges in the MODERATELY SELECTIVE category	
Accept fewer than 70% of all applicants, Average combined SAT (CR + M) 1110+, Average composite ACT 24+	
Appalachian State University	Pepperdine University
Augustana College (IL)	Purdue University
Baylor University	Rochester Institute of Technology
Beloit College	Rollins College
Bennington College	Sarah Lawrence College
Butler University	Sewanee – University of the South
CUNY Baruch	St. Lawrence University
California Polytechnic State U (SLO)	Texas Christian University
Centre College	The College of New Jersey
Chapman University	The College of Wooster
Clark University	Trinity College
Clarkson University	Trinity University
DePauw University	United States Coast Guard Academy
Drake University	University of California – San Diego
Earlham College	University of California – Santa Barbara
Elon University	University of Connecticut
Florida International University	University of Dayton
Florida State University	University of Delaware
George Mason University	University of Illinois at Urbana-Champaign
Gonzaga University	University of Maryland-Baltimore County
Gustavus Adolphus College	University of Massachusetts-Amherst
Hampshire College	University of North Carolina at Asheville
Illinois Institute of Technology	University of Portland
Illinois Wesleyan University	University of San Diego
Kalamazoo University	University of South Carolina
Kettering University	University of Texas at Austin
Lewis & Clark College	University of Texas at Dallas
Loyola Marymount University	University of Tulsa
Loyola University of Maryland	University of Washington
Marquette University	University of Wisconsin-Madison
Miami University	Ursinus College
Milwaukee School of Engineering	Virginia Tech
Muhlenberg College	Washington College
New College of Florida	Wheaton College (IL)
North Carolina State University	Wheaton College (MA)
Penn State University	

3.2 CONSIDERATIONS FOR CHOOSING COLLEGES

There are many things to consider when choosing colleges. The questions below will help you start thinking about what is important to you for your college experience:

- Do you have a location in mind for college, e.g., specific city, state, or region?
- Do you have a preference for climate?
- Do you want to be near home and family or relatives?
- Do you prefer a city, suburb, small town, or rural location?
- Do you want your college to be near other colleges, i.e. in a college town?
- Do you parents have a specific location in mind?
- Will you consider locations you don't yet know, or do you prefer locations you know?
- What are your academic interests?
- Do you have a specific career in mind?
- What college major do you think best suits that career?
- Do you have any other academic interests that you would like to pursue in college?
- Do you like the challenge of difficult classes and competitive classmates, or do you prefer being at the top of a less competitive group?
- How hard do you work in high school? And how hard do you want to work in college?

With your responses in mind, now consider the following:

Academic Program
You can start to narrow your search immediately if you know what you want to study. For example, if you are interested in engineering programs, then choose a college that has a solid and prestigious engineering program. If you are undecided about mechanical or electrical engineering, for example, don't worry at this stage – just choosing a college with a solid engineering program is a great start. Remember, it is always possible to change your major, but choosing schools on the basis of the academic program can be a good first step.

Cost
Cost is a very important factor and you need to how your education is being funded. If you are fortunate to have your parents helping out, you need first to discuss finances with them and find out what they – and/or you – are able to spend. Once that is established, you will need to consider if you need to take out a loan and the implications of that. Knowing your financial situation may influence your choice of colleges. For example, although the price tag on private schools is high, they offer opportunities to apply and receive financial help through scholarships. They also offer a better chance of obtaining the classes you need, meaning that the probability of completing a Bachelor's degree in the allotted four-year time frame is better than with a state institution where popular classes can be impacted (over-subscribed). Consider also, the cost-effective option of starting your college studies at a junior college and transferring to a four-year private or state college to complete your degree.

Location of Campus
Location is an important consideration. Do you want/need to be close to home or are you excited about going somewhere completely different? As you build your college list, it can be exciting to imagine yourself away from home, living an independent life with no responsibilities, but, also, it can be a little daunting and you might feel that you are not ready for that distance yet. It is a very good idea to attend an open event if possible and, if you can arrange it, an overnight visit on the campus of a school you really think

you love so that you can take a look around and get a feel for the environment. It will also give you a chance to meet other students and see how they cope with student life.

Weather
For some students, weather is not a consideration, but for others it is a priority. Think about the kind of activities you like to do and if or how the weather impacts your enjoyment of them.

Greek Life
Many students consider belonging to a Sorority or Fraternity a very important part of their decision-making process. It is important to understand that, although you may want to join one of these societies, they also have their own separate entry process and, as such, there is no guarantee that you will be admitted into one of them. There is also a financial consideration to being a member of these societies. One way to help decide if a school is right for you is to ask yourself if you would still like the school if you were not a direct part of Greek life.

Environment
This is a very important factor for most students. Do you want to be in your home state? Or would you prefer to go to another part of the country (or world) to experience a completely different environment? Considerations for this decision include whether or not you want:

- A rural or urban campus;
- A fast or slow-paced lifestyle;
- A college town environment;
- A natural environment for activities you enjoy (skiing, surfing, etc.).

Some colleges are integral to the communities of the city or town in which they are situated. Some colleges have excellent connections with local businesses that enable students to participate in internships and work experience activities. Some colleges work with local volunteer groups and offer opportunities for students to actively contribute to a variety of causes. If things like this are important to you, research colleges that offer the opportunities you want. Try to go to an open event at the college if possible.

College Rankings
College rankings are useful, but should not be your sole means of evaluating a school's potential as a 'fit' for you. Although it may be tempting to apply only to the best colleges, try not to set too much store by the various college rankings. The high-ranking colleges are prestigious and challenging and are not the 'best fit' choices for every student.

Size of School
The size of a college is an important aspect of the college experience and when choosing colleges, it is worth considering the following:

> ***Size of Classes*** - A college's size often affects the size of its classes. In general, larger schools tend to have larger classes, especially at freshman level. Introductory classes in large schools may have a hundred or more students in one class. At smaller schools you will have smaller class sizes, closer contact with the professor and other students, and increased opportunities to participate. If you have a preference for a particular style of learning, this can be a factor to consider as you research colleges.

Graduation Statistics – Depending on the size of the school, and particularly in large public schools, it can be difficult to get the classes you want – and need – when you want them. This means that you may have to wait to get those classes and, if you have not fulfilled the required course load for your degree, you cannot graduate until you have done so. It is not uncommon for undergraduates at large public schools to take six years or more to graduate. When considering a school, therefore, and particularly if finances are a concern, it is advisable to investigate the graduation statistics (often measured in terms of percentage of students graduating within 6 years).

Interactions with Faculty - Not all teachers and professors offer the same experience to their students and the size of college is often a factor in this. Large universities often have professors who are considered senior-level in their field of research. As such, these professors spend a lot of time working on research, projects, and publications that enhance their reputation within the academic field as well as the college's reputation for excellence in that field. Undergraduates may not have much contact with these professors: they may lecture, but it will be teaching assistants (graduate students) doing the majority of the teaching and grading. At smaller colleges, particularly those with no graduate programs, there is less likelihood of there being 'big-name' professors, but there is a greater chance that you will be taught by professors and that you will have greater interaction with them. Many small colleges pride themselves on the mentoring-type relationships between professors and students.

Extracurricular Activities - The size of a college can have a big impact on extracurricular activities. Typically, the larger the college, the larger variety of activities offered. This means that if you are interested in a relatively obscure activity, there is more chance you will find it – or something related to it – at a larger school. On the other hand, if you are interested in one of the more popular activities on a larger campus, it may be difficult to get involved. At smaller colleges, students may have less choice of extracurricular activities but they will often find it easier to get involved.

Social Life - Just as with extracurricular activities, larger schools generally have a greater variety of social options than smaller schools. Larger schools also offer a wider student participation in any one event (such as the huge turnouts on game day). Smaller schools may seem friendlier, mostly because you will run into the same people more often and you will have a smaller number of choices of places to go and things to do. However, a more intimate atmosphere happens in larger schools too: Once you get settled into a dorm, a department, and a routine of activities that you enjoy, your social life and friend group will naturally evolve into a smaller and more comfortable environment.

Study Abroad Programs - Many colleges offer study abroad opportunities, either for an entire academic year, a semester, or just a few weeks. By studying abroad, students gain a wealth of experience, develop a global perspective, hone foreign language skills, discover a different side of their academic study, and benefit from international networking experience. These are all benefits that can translate into real job skills after graduation. Many schools offer unusual and exciting opportunities beyond the more familiar European study abroad experience. If studying abroad interests you, research colleges that offer opportunities for the experience you want.

Diversity - One of the most exciting aspects of college life is the opportunity to meet people from all walks of life and from all over the country and the world. Diversity enhances every campus in its natural promotion of expansive and global thinking.

Social Consciousness - Every generation sets out to make changes to their world. College offers unparalleled opportunities to learn about social and humanitarian issues and ideas about how to make meaningful change for the better. In all fields of academic study, from engineering to politics, colleges offer students opportunities to focus on problems; how to evaluate them, understand them, and solve them. Whatever your field of study, if you want to 'change the world', look for schools that make it their mission to find ways to make the world a better place.

'Special' programs – As you research colleges, make note of the programs, classes, awards, and other 'special' aspects. You might find these on a college's website, promoted under headings such as:

- Centers of Excellence
- Points of Distinction
- Points of Pride
- Unique Opportunities
- Specialized Programs
- Rankings and Awards
- Publications, Debates, Podcasts, Documentaries
- TED Talks
- Peace Corps Volunteers
- Global Programs
- President's Higher Education Community Service Honor Roll

Careers Center

It is useful to think about what happens *after* college. Large universities may have career centers in every department and smaller liberal arts schools may have one centralized office. The quality of information available and help offered in career guidance will differ from school to school and major to major. A good way to determine the strength of a college's Career Center is to look at its facilities, and in particular on:

- Calendar of events for career search, internships, and networking opportunities throughout the school year;
- Placement Statistics – information on employers that have recently hired graduates and results on alumni placement;
- Special programs – specialized programs dedicated to preparing students for careers are useful resources;
- Support for National Fellowships and Scholarships, such as Rhodes Scholars and Watson Fellowships, are coordinated through the career center;
- Career apps are devised and used by some colleges to provide information on upcoming events, job openings, and information on job search strategies;
- Cooperative Programs offer students the opportunity to alternate classes with actual work at a participating business where they are paid a salary. These are available mostly for engineering and business programs and are valuable experiences that prepare a student for the real world.

Scholarships

Many schools have a variety of scholarships based on different criteria. Some scholarships have an open application policy, which means that students are automatically evaluated for scholarship when they submit their application. Other scholarships may require a separate application, some based on the quality of the applicant in the initial application, and some based on an applicant's choice of major or stated area of interest. Some college websites will have one central list of scholarships available, whilst others may disperse the information by department. It is worthwhile taking a closer look for scholarships for which you may be eligible.

Cross Registration

College consortiums offer students the opportunity to take classes at participating colleges through a cross registration system. Students are 'based' in one college, from which they will earn their degree, but can take classes in any of the consortium member colleges. Some of the well-known consortiums are:

- The Five College Consortium consisting of Amherst, Hampshire, Mount Holyoke, Smith, and the University of Massachusetts;
- The Claremont Colleges consisting of Claremont-McKenna, Scripps, Harvey Mudd, Pomona, and Pitzer;
- The Quaker consortium consisting of Bryn Mawr, Haverford, and Swarthmore.

In consortiums, each school maintains separate admissions, tuition, and graduation requirements and each will have rules regarding the number of classes that a student can take at member institutions, e.g. one a semester, a total number in a year, or a total number in the degree program.

3.3 TYPES OF EDUCATIONAL INSTITUTIONS

There are thousands of higher-level educational institutions in the United States and, whilst no two are exactly alike, the majority fit into one or more of the categories listed below:

LIBERAL ARTS COLLEGES

These schools focus on undergraduate education and the professors who teach at these schools consider teaching their primary responsibility. Liberal arts colleges offer an education that encompasses the arts. A liberal arts education allows students to explore a variety of academic subjects, with at least one area of in-depth study that is their college 'major'. Unlike a subject-focused major in Nursing, Accounting, or Engineering that follows a stringent rubric of required classes and prepares a student for a career in a specific field, a liberal arts education is not career specific. A student with a Liberal Arts undergraduate degree is prepared for a career in a variety of fields.

UNIVERSITIES

These schools are generally larger and include a liberal arts college, as well as various colleges focused on education in specific fields related to specific careers, such as Nursing, Education, Engineering, etc. Universities offer a greater range of academic choices than liberal arts colleges, but the classes can often be larger too. The scope of research opportunities and other extracurricular options can be vast and readily available.

SPECIALIZED SCHOOLS - TECHNICAL INSTITUTES, CAREER SCHOOLS/PROFESSIONAL SCHOOLS

These schools are targeted towards students who have made clear decisions about what they want to study and they emphasize preparation for specific careers. Technical institutes emphasize preparation for careers in engineering and technical services, and professional schools (such as art and design colleges and music schools) focus on specific careers in fine arts, design, and music.

HISTORICALLY BLACK COLLEGES AND UNIVERSITIES
These schools originated during a time when African-American students were denied access to most other colleges and universities. Students at these schools have the opportunity to experience an academic community in which they are part of the majority and are encouraged in their expectations of success.

TRIBAL COLLEGES
These colleges focus on the educational needs, aspirations, and success of American-Indian students.

WOMEN'S COLLEGES
These colleges feature larger numbers of female faculty and administrators and offer women greater opportunities for student leadership and a focused approach to career possibilities for women. Women's colleges have a high number of Science majors and students who continue to graduate school and/or professional studies.

RELIGIOUS-AFFILIATION COLLEGES AND UNIVERSITIES
Formed by religious groups and organizations, these academic institutions were principally focused on aligning education with religious principles. Although they are not limited in admission to members of that religious group, these schools will often require students take one or two religion classes (sometimes more) as part of their core curriculum.

COMMUNITY OR JUNIOR COLLEGES
These generally offer the first two years of a liberal arts education in additional to specialized occupational preparation. At the successful completion of two years of study, a student is awarded an Associate Degree. Many students continue their education at a four-year institution through a transfer process.

3.4 MAJORS, MINORS, AND 'AREAS OF INTEREST'

A Major
A major is a specific subject in which you choose to specialize. Typically, between a third and a half of the classes you will take in college will be related to your major. Some colleges offer other options: a double major (by which you study two subjects in equal depth), a major-minor combination (the minor being a specialization that requires fewer classes than the major), or a major of your own creation (which requires academic approval from the college).

Although you may not need to 'declare' a major on your college application (unless you are interested in medicine, law, or architecture, for example), you may be required to indicate an area of academic interest. Whatever you put down will not be deciding your fate; it simply enables the admissions officers to see your academic 'leaning,' which ultimately helps him or her decide on the make-up and balance of the freshman class.

When to Choose a Major
At most four-year colleges, and in the case of many majors, you choose your major at the end of sophomore year. This gives you time to explore different subjects and decide which are of interest. There are two main exceptions to this rule: 1) Some majors, such as those in specialized areas of engineering, must be declared earlier as more time is required to fulfill all the requirements; and 2) if you are studying on a two-year degree program, you will probably select a major at the start of your freshman year because the program is much shorter.

How to Choose a Major

One way to choose a major is to choose a subject that interests and motivates you. One thing that may stop you doing this is concern that you don't know what you will do with it after college (i.e. you love creative writing, but you know that the life of a writer is solitary and you would prefer to work with people). The point to remember is that, by indicating an 'area of interest,' you are indicating to the admissions officers your potential for completing an area of study in this field, and <u>not</u> necessarily pursuing a career in it. Some questions to ask yourself when considering your interests, skills, and abilities for indicating your major or an area of academic interest on your application include:

- In which subjects do I have the highest grades?
- Why do I have the highest grades in this subject? (I like the teacher, I really understand the material, etc.)
- How do I feel about doing homework in this subject?
- Do I like being 'good' at this subject?
- Does it interest me?
- Do I want to know more about this subject?

If you have no idea of a major, it is perfectly acceptable to be 'undeclared' and discover the right one for you after exploring different subjects. But, it is worth considering for the purpose of your application that, when you are being considered against students with similar grades, some schools may view the student with obvious interests and even a vague idea of direction as the more appealing, mature, and focused candidate than the student with no idea at all.

You Can Change Your Mind

If you're not sure about your college major while you're in high school, don't worry. Many students switch their major during college. Even students who are convinced of the major they want to take often change their mind.

Majors and Graduate School

Some colleges offer pre-professional advisory programs — such as premed or prelaw — to students who plan on attending medical school, law school, or graduate school. These programs are not the same as majors and you will still need to choose a major. Students who are planning to continue their education in professional or graduate programs often choose a major related to their future field. For example, undergraduates in premed programs will likely choose to major in biology or chemistry, but they do not have to do so. For a student to continue their studies, they need to fulfill the course requirements of the program they want to enter, and can major in any subject they like.

Majors and Professions

If you major in a specific area, such as nursing, accounting or engineering, you are preparing for a career in those specific fields. Many majors, however, prepare you to apply to a variety of careers once you graduate. For example, a degree in English Literature is a suitable qualification for applications to jobs in all type of fields, including, publishing, advertising, teaching, public relations, or law. Similarly, a degree in psychology is a suitable qualification for applications for jobs in human resources, education, sales, and a vast array of careers requiring strong interpersonal skills.

Declaring an 'Area of Interest' on the College Application
Although it is not often required for you to declare a major on your college application, many schools ask for your 'Area of interest.' Don't be alarmed! This is not a formal declaration of a major; it is simply a way for colleges to understand your 'leaning' toward a specific subject area. This information helps college admissions officers build a balanced class of students with a range of interests and abilities.

3.5 ROTC (Reserve Officers' Training Corps)

ROTC is a specialized program to train college students for future service in branches of the U.S. military; the Army, Navy and Marines and the Air Force, each of which have their own programs. High school students interested in U.S. Armed Forces can also gain exposure to military training through JROTC (Junior ROTC) programs. JROTC programs provide students with at least three years of military instruction, along with access to uniforms, academic materials, and instructors who have served as U.S. Armed Forces officers. According to numbers published by the U.S. Army, over 274,000 high school students serve as JROTC cadets.

At college, the goal of these specific college-level programs is to train future officers to serve in the U.S. Armed Forces. To students who qualify, the ROTC programs offer scholarships that cover the cost of their education. In return, students are obliged to fulfill active duty services in their chosen branch of the Armed Forces. The table below outlines the programs and related information. Further details on the ROTC can be found on: www.todaysmilitary.com.

	TYPES OF ROTC PROGRAMS		
	Army	**Navy and Marine Corps**	**Air Force**
Availability	1,100 campus programs	153 campus programs	1,100 campus programs
Example Training Topics	Army leadership, military tactics, principles of war, and combat survival training.	Summer cruise training, surface warfare orientation, flight time on navy aircraft, and maritime self-defense.	Laws of armed conflict, international security, aerospace studies, and field training.
Service Obligations	3-8 years, depending on scholarship acceptance.	Between 3-12 years of active military service, depending on scholarship acceptance and degree level.	Between 4-10 years of active duty, depending on contract cadet appointment.
Example Career Specialties	Infantry, Military Intelligence, Civil Affairs, Medical Corps.	Submarine, Explosive Ordinance Disposal, US Marine Corps, Navy Nursing Corps.	Air Battle Management, Aircraft Maintenance, Cyberspace Operations, Piloting, and Tactical Air Control.

3.6 COLLEGE SEARCH RESOURCES

There are many resources available that range from highly subjective opinions about the schools you are considering to more objective descriptions about a school's programs and philosophies. Just like any research project, it's a good idea to surround yourself with a variety of sources from both ends of the spectrum so that you may ultimately form your own opinion about a college and make an informed decision about whether it's right for you. Resources include:

HIGH SCHOOL COUNSELORS
School counselors are one of the best sources of support for students applying to college. They can guide students in their research, help them build an appropriate list, and advocate for them during the college process. It is worth getting to know your counselor early on in high school; the more the counselor knows

about you and your interests and abilities, the more they are able to help you. Counselors can help students:

- Plan classes that prepare you for college admission and success;
- Review your academic record and suggest areas of improvement;
- Help in early stages of college process by identifying the questions you should be asking;
- Clarify terms that you will encounter during the college process;
- Identify special opportunities that may maximize your potential as a college applicant;
- Assist in registering for college admission tests, such as SAT and ACT;
- Secure applications, identify deadlines, and prioritize tasks you need to complete during the process;
- Polish your applications and any required college essays so that they are representative of you and your abilities;
- Explore options for financing college;
- Identify appropriate scholarships;
- Provide a letter of recommendation;
- Compare offers of admission and financial aid.

Questions that your high school counselor can answer include:

- What courses do I need to take to be ready for college?
- How should I plan my schedule so I will complete them?
- Which elective courses do you recommend?
- Which AP courses should I consider taking?
- When is the PSAT/NMSQT going to be given?
- How should I study for the SAT, and is it given at this high school or do I need to go somewhere nearby?
- Are there any college planning sessions scheduled?
- Are there college handbooks or other guides that I can browse or borrow?
- What activities can I do at home and over the summer to get ready for college?
- What kinds of grades do different colleges require?
- Are there any college fairs at this school, or nearby?
- What colleges do other students from our school go to?
- What are the requirements or standards for the honor programs/society?
- Can you put me in touch with recent graduates who are going to the colleges on my wish list?
- Do you have any information to help me start exploring careers?
- If my colleges need a recommendation from you, how can I help you know me better, so it can be more personal?
- Are there any special scholarships or awards that I should know about now, so I can start working towards them?
- How does our school compare to others, in terms of test scores and reputation?
- What forms do I need for financial aid?

PRIVATE / INDEPENDENT COLLEGE COUNSELOR
Private college counselors offer personalized service to help a student through all aspects of the college applications process. This often includes learning about a student's academic, career, and personal aspirations and then making suggestions on colleges and class choices and preparing an academic plan. They may also make recommendations on extracurricular activities, school clubs, and volunteer opportunities to suit a student's personality and direction. Private counselors advise freshmen and

sophomores on the best classes and tests to help them get into their preferred schools. For juniors, they offer advice and honest feedback on college choices, will draw up a plan for fulfilling the application requirements for each college, and will guide and support the student through every part of the application, including offering advice on all stages of the admissions essays.

When considering a private counselor, it is useful to think first about your academic goals. If you want to apply to highly selective colleges, a private counselor can guide you through the complexities of their requirements and potentially improve your chances of acceptance. If you are applying to specialized colleges (for art, drama, or music, for example), a private college counselor can be helpful in guiding you through the specific requirements, such as portfolio submission, targeted essay subjects, and audition techniques.

A private college counselor may also be a good choice for students with uncommon educational backgrounds. Homeschooled and international students who have studied a different curriculum and have different qualifications and records may benefit from a private counselor's expertise. Students with learning differences and students who have changed schools or have missed a significant number of school days may also need additional help when applying for college. Private counselors can help a student and family stay focused and on track with essential deadlines.

It is advisable to meet with a potential private college counselor face-to-face before committing to a service, and ask about:

- The counselor's qualifications – degree level, counseling and/or educational counseling certification and registration with reputable organizations;
- The counselor's track record and the schools to which their students were admitted;
- The counselor's current commitments - you don't want to hire a counselor who is so full of commitments that the student cannot meet with him or her regularly;
- An outline of the counselor's process;
- An explanation of the counselor's services, including class selection, test advice, tutoring, etc;
- A sense of the counselor's personality to ensure a good fit.

NAVIANCE

Naviance is a comprehensive college preparation guide for students, parents, counselors, and teachers to use throughout the college application process. It is a useful tool and valuable information resource for students and parents and a channel of communication between the high school college counselor and families.

The 'Family Connection' Home page is a message board from the counselors in your school. It will give important dates of in-house meetings about colleges, finance, scholarships, application dates for state schools, and other relevant information. Also listed are links to state universities, the Common Application and other applications, and financial aid information. Naviance provides an enormous amount of information, the most relevant at this stage of the college search being:

COLLEGE SEARCH

A good way to start is to complete the college search profile under the 'College Super Match' tab. There are over 20 sections to help you focus on what you want out of your college experience and, from your responses, schools that match your criteria will be listed. Although there are many unknowns at the beginning of your search, it is worthwhile making a start and familiarizing yourself with the content.

Within each section is one constant question: "How important is this to you?" to which the responses are 'Kinda', 'Very', or 'Must Have.' This means that if you say that you want to go to schools in California, for example, and then indicate its importance to you as a 'Must Have' your matches will show only colleges in California. The criteria you can enter to narrow down your search are vast, and include:

Location	Indicate preference by region and/or state
Majors	Indicate type of degree (Bachelors or Associate) and the Major
My Scores	SAT (1600 or 2400), ACT, and Unweighted GPA. You can also express interest in schools with an Open Admissions Policy and schools where you would be well above average and could therefore increase your financial aid opportunities
Tuition & Fees	Sliding scale up to $50,000 per year on which you indicate the amount per year you can pay for tuition. You can also indicate your home state for base rates
Ethnicity	Campus diversity and preference for specific representation (African American, Hispanic, Asian, Native American, Caucasian)
School Type	Traditional 4-year college/university or Community/Technical 2-year college
Size of School	Very large - Over 20,000 students Large - 13,001 to 20,000 students Mid-size - 7,000 to 13,000 students Small - 2,0001 to 7,000 Very small - 2,000 or fewer students
On Campus Housing	Indicate if you wish to have on-campus housing
Campus Setting	Large urban area – Population more than 250,000 Small urban area – Population less than 250,000 Suburb/town close to a large urban area Suburb/town close to a small urban area Rural
Public or Private	Indicate preference
Gender Mix	Coed, Female-only, Male-only
Historically Black	Indicate preference
	Very Selective - admits less than 1/3 of applicants Selective - admits 1/3 to 2/3 of applicants Wide Open - admits over 2/3 of applicants
Graduation Rate	Indicate if you have preference to attend a college from which most students graduate
Organizations	Indicate interests in academic and special interests clubs: political, religious, and cultural organizations; and music, media, and environmental groups
Special Services	Indicate preference for schools that offer remedial, academic/career counseling, and job placement services
Disability Services	Preference for school that offers services for mobility, visually, or hearing impaired
Sports	Preference for colleges with varsity teams in sport of your choice and division of your choice
Greek Life	Preference for 1) interest in joining a sorority/fraternity, or 2) attending a school without Greek Life
Religious Affiliation	Indicate preference for school with particular belief system (Christian, Jewish, or Other) and preference for particular religious affiliation within belief system
Liberal-Conservative	Preference for the political/cultural/social climate of the college
LGBT-Friendly	Preference for schools with strong support systems for gay, lesbian, bisexual, and transgender students
Great College Towns	Indicate preference for school located in a great college town

CHOOSING COLLEGES

COLLEGE MATCH & COLLEGE COMPARE

Once you have completed the questionnaire in Super Match, you can move to the College Match tab and there will be a list that match the criteria you indicated. Remember, the more responses you give, the more valuable this list will be because it will provide schools that match ALL your criteria. From this list you can choose to:

- Add to the 'Colleges I'm thinking about;'
- Link to the college's website for more information on admission, etc.;
- Indicate that you are 'not interested.'

In the College Compare section, you can compare up to ten colleges against each other and in relation to YOUR grades (High School GPA or International Baccalaureate grade and PSAT, SAT, and ACT scores).

COLLEGE LOOKUP

In this section you can search for colleges by categories, such as

- Name;
- Group, e.g. colleges that use the Common Application, or Ivy League;
- Country or US state.

You will be directed to that particular college's profile page, which shows information on:

- Cost, with links to information on Cost and Aid;
- Graduation rate within a stated number of years;
- Acceptance rate - with a direct link to your personal Scattergram – a two-axis graph that presents qualifications of students who were admitted, waitlisted, or rejected in previous years and indication of where your qualifications fit into the admissions profile of that college;
- Information on college overlaps - names of colleges to which students who applied to this particular college also applied;)
- Admission deadlines;
- Information on how a student's standardized test scores (SAT and/or ACT) compare with students from the student's own high school and with students nationally.

COLLEGE RESOURCES and COLLEGE MAPS

College Resources provides direct links to information on:

- Colleges and Careers
- Financial Aid
- Test Preparation
- College Athletics
- Military (ROTC)

College Maps provides information on the schools to which students from your high school have applied, with information on acceptances from your high school and a list of the top 20 most popular colleges for students from your high school. There are also maps for groups of colleges, including:

- 100 Hidden Gems;
- Colleges that a particular year of your high school attended;
- Community Colleges;
- Private Schools within your state;
- Colleges that use the Common Application;
- Historically Black colleges, Hispanic-serving colleges, Ivy League, Jesuit colleges, and Catholic colleges.

SCATTERGRAMS and ACCEPTANCE HISTORY

In this section you can see how your qualifications compare to the qualifications of accepted students. As long as you have your correct test scores in the system, you will appear on the scattergram as a little blue circle and you can see where you are in relation to students who have been accepted, wait-listed, and rejected. The Acceptance History section provides data on colleges to which students from your high school have been accepted and enrolled.

TRANSCRIPTS

In this section, you will find direct links to request transcripts for college applications, scholarships, and athletics, as well as a link to status report on requested, sent, or pending transcripts

TEST SCORES

This section lists all the scores from the tests you have taken: PSAT, SAT, ACT, SAT Subject tests, AP, and, where applicable, the TOEFL (Test of English as a Foreign Language).

OTHER IMPORTANT RESOURCES INCLUDE:

COLLEGE WEBSITES

College websites offer a wealth of information and are often more current than college view books. They provide important data, including admissions criteria, department listings, student organizations, alumni networks, and information on current research. Combined with the photographs (and sometimes videos), college websites are a great way to 'visit' the school and get a sense of whether it is somewhere you would like to consider.

COLLEGE FAIRS

Across the country, the spring college fairs are the ideal venues to investigate schools you may be considering but don't know too much about. Use the opportunity to speak with admissions officers from schools that might be difficult for you to visit. It's also a good idea to meet representatives from those schools to which you plan to apply. To make the most of your college fair experience, these pointers might help:

Before the Fair:

- Consider what you are looking for in a school—big/small, major, urban/rural, 2-year/4-year, religiously-affiliation, athletics, Greek life, special programs/opportunities, etc;

CHOOSING COLLEGES

- Make a list of schools that are a "must" to connect with. You may not be able to get to every college, so know ahead of time what type of colleges you would be interested in attending;
- If you can, register online ahead of time. You will be given a bar code that the college representative will be able to scan to get your contact information;
- Have a professional email address for all college correspondence;
- Have some questions ready for college representatives, especially those in which you are most interested - this will generate interesting and specific conversations.

During the Fair:

- Get there early - these fairs can be VERY busy;
- Bring a pen, paper, and tote bag for notes and materials;
- Take a map (if available) – highlight the schools you want to visit and plan your route.
- Be patient—you may have to wait in line to talk to a college representative;
- If your parents attend with you, ask them to let you talk to the college representative, but do listen to their ideas and suggestions too;
- Take notes! Write down what you find most interesting about each college;
- Ask for business cards. Follow up with the rep if you have more questions or just want to thank them for their time;
- Be adventurous! Chat with representatives from colleges you may not have considered or heard of;
- Attend an information session to learn more about the college search process, financial aid, and other topics.

After the Fair:

- Organize and sort through all of the material you have collected;
- Make notes about schools that stood out to you while it is fresh in your mind;
- To help narrow your choices, review college websites, catalogs, and view books of the schools that interested you most;
- Make a note of additional questions you have and want to follow up on;
- Send a 'nice to meet you' thank you email to the college representative. This simple gesture can show admission officials you are serious about wanting to attend their college;
- Talk to your parents and counselor about what schools peaked your interest and why;
- Adjust your college list accordingly, if necessary;
- Start scheduling visits to your top schools;
- Read e-mails to see when colleges will be visiting your school or community.

College fairs are a great resource during the college search process. Plan ahead and get the most out of your experience. Enjoy!

COLLEGE REPRESENTATIVE VISITS TO HIGH SCHOOLS

Admissions representatives from colleges nationwide visit schools all over the nation. These visits are a great way to learn more about a school and to speak with a representative from a college in which you are interested but haven't been able to visit. This is the time to express your interest to the admissions officers and to make sure that they have your name on file (and that you have their name and contact details).

GETTING THROUGH IT TOGETHER

BOOKS, WEBSITES, 'BEST OF...' LISTS AND BOOKS, RANKINGS

There are myriad resources available that range from highly subjective opinions to objective descriptions about a school's programs and philosophy. Details of resources that provide valuable information are in the Resources section of this book. Remember, things change, and it is important to always research the school for the latest information relating to requirements, costs, etc.

FAMILY, FRIENDS, TEACHERS – YOUR PERSONAL CONTACT LIST

Once you start asking the question, "Where did you go to college?" you will start to hear the names of all sorts of colleges you didn't know and therefore hadn't thought about. Start asking family, friends, teachers, and people you admire where they went to college and keep a log of the information as a starting point for further research. Depending on your interests, you could start to formulate a list into categories and put in schools that meet those interests. A log could look like the table below:

College Names Log			
Ivy league	**Friends discuss**	**In-state schools**	**Grandparents like**
Brown	Stanford	UC Berkeley	LMU
Cornell	Duke	UCLA	U San Diego
Dartmouth	Georgetown	UC Davis	Pepperdine
	NYU		
Family	**Friends**	**Teachers**	**Counselors**
U San Diego (Dad)	Miami Ohio (Caroline)	Brown (Ms. Jones)	Cal Poly (Ms. Diaz)
U Washington (Mom)	SMU (Meg)	Northwestern (Mr. Hill)	Elon U (Ms. Brown)
Rutgers (cousin)	Chapman (Olivia)	Baylor (Coach Stevens)	Tulane (Mr. O)
Carnegie Mellon (Liz)	Purdue (Thomas)	San Fran State (Ms. P)	
Vanderbilt (Aunt Grace)	Ithaca (Liam)	Davidson (Ms. J)	
Specialized			**Sports**
U Arizona	Astronomy	Wellesley	Ice Hockey
Otterbein	Drama	Amherst	
New School	Design/Art	Union	

3.7 COLLEGE VISITS

Once you have completed some preliminary research, you should have some idea of the schools you want to know about and the schools that you would like to visit if possible. Visiting colleges has many advantages, the most important of which can be:

1. You will get a 'feel' for the campus, the students, the academic departments, and specific areas and opportunities that interest you;
2. You can potentially meet with faculty and admissions representatives and indicate to them your interest in the school;
3. Build a portfolio of schools that you can refer to when you need to make a decision.

CHOOSING COLLEGES

When to Visit
Admissions offices are open all year, but visiting when classes are in session is best. If you visit in the summer, you will get to walk around the campus and learn about admissions, but it will be difficult to get a sense of the atmosphere of the college. The best time to visit schools is in spring break of junior year. Even if you have not finalized your list, it's a good idea to try and see at least one large, one medium size, and one small school and you will be better prepared to make decisions about where to apply.

Once you have finalized your list and/or have applied, you could return to schools for an overnight visit. On these visits, you can be a college student for the day; attend classes, eat in the cafeteria and interact with students. For all visits, check the college websites or call the admissions office for more information.

Planning a Visit
A good campus visit takes between two and four hours and, allowing another hour or so to explore the town and/or surrounding area, you should probably aim to visit no more than two schools in a day. To make the most of every school visit:

- Call the admissions office at least two weeks ahead of time to schedule your visit. At this time you should also let them know if you would like to sit in on a particular class, meet a particular professor, or talk with an advisor;
- Request an interview if the school offers on-campus interviews. A word of advice to the painfully shy, tongue-tied, or extremely anxious student, I suggest you speak to your counselor before scheduling an interview if you think that it might put you at a disadvantage;
- If you have a particular area of interest or expertise, or you know the major(s) you want to pursue, you might want to contact the appropriate department, coach, or professor and ask if they are available on the day of your visit;
- Contact anyone you or your parents know who are current students or alumni of the school you're visiting. They are the best source for the 'inside scoop', but do remember that their opinions are based on their experiences and you should try to remain objective;
- Many colleges offer overnight visits for prospective students. Some colleges set aside specific weekends (usually in the spring) and others will arrange a visit to suit your timetable. The best times to visit are, either, before applications are due, or after you've accepted. No student has time (or should have time!) to spend a night at ten different colleges, so it is better to plan a visit after you have narrowed down your list. One good strategy is to visit two schools that you like that are completely different (for example, a big urban university and a small rural college). By doing this, you will get a very good idea of what kind of environment and community suits you best. If you're thinking of applying Early Decision, an overnight visit is essential. Spend as much time as possible on campus to make sure that the school is your absolute first choice. As with all college visits, you will need to call the admissions office a few weeks (or maybe even months) ahead of time. Ask if overnight visits are an option and then plan a date. If you have family traveling with you, the admissions office will probably be able to offer advice on where they can stay;
- Make notes immediately after your visit. **The template at the end of this section is a guide on the things to look for and questions to ask during those visits.** Whatever format you use, it's a good idea to keep a comprehensive record of each visit, the people you meet, and features that you want to remember. If you are visiting several schools, you will find these notes invaluable when you start to pull together your list.

Day of Your Visit
If you have planned ahead, you will probably have a full schedule, but if certain things have not been arranged and if you have time, try to:

- Attend one of the school's general information sessions;
- Sit in on a class (or two);
- Talk to a professor (or even a student) in your chosen major;
- Talk to a coach in your chosen sport;
- Talk to a student or counselor in the career center;
- Wander around the campus by yourself;
- Eat in the cafeteria;
- Talk to students: ask why they chose this college and their favorite aspects of it. Ask them what they do on weekends;
- Read the student newspaper, even the advertisements;
- **Take a look at the student notice boards for information on events, music, sports activities, clubs, and organizations;**
- Read bulletin boards of department(s) in which you are interested. Look for information on events, competitions, research opportunities, study abroad programs, etc;
- Walk or drive around the area surrounding the campus;
- Find out how students get around: public transport, bike, or walk;
- Visit the career center and ask about job opportunities;
- Browse in the bookstore.

The Overnight Visit
When you pack for your overnight visit, take your college file and some homework with you. You will probably have some time on your own whilst your host studies or attends class and you can use that time to make notes on the college and get your homework done.

When you arrive on campus, you will probably be escorted on a tour, attend an interview or information session at the admission office, and participate in activities that the school arranges as part of the scheduled visit. You will be introduced to your student host and the overnight experience will begin. Of course, your experience depends a lot on the college and your student host, but it will be enhanced if you are open minded and positive. Be friendly and try to meet as many students as you can. You will have time to do most of the activities suggested above, and you might have the opportunity to check out other aspects of the campus, such as:

- Favorite hangouts;
- The social scene (especially if it's a weekend visit);
- See a lecture, play, music event, or other campus-wide event;
- Ask several different students a lot of questions, such as:

    Why did you choose this college?
    What is your favorite part of being at college?
    What do you do at weekends?
    How many hours do you study per week?
    How many times do you go home during the school year?
    What student groups are the most active?
    What does a typical weekday look like?
    What don't you like about this college?

Etiquette during and after your visit

"You never get a second chance to make a first impression!" Think of your school visit as an interview and treat everyone you meet as though they are in some way connected to the admissions process. This means that you should dress appropriately, conduct yourself in a positive manner, and treat everyone with respect: from your initial handshake or greeting, to your full attention during tours and sessions, to your final thank you and goodbye. Good manners, respect, and a positive attitude are the best ways to be remembered and appreciated.

After your visit, it is a good idea to send a note or brief email of thanks to the person who interviewed you and any person who took the time to meet with you. It cannot be stressed enough that good manners are always remembered and appreciated.

Communicating with colleges

Whenever you contact the admissions office of any school to which you are applying, assume that your phone call, email, or letter is recorded and added to your file. Make sure that every communication is concise and well presented. When you contact an admissions officer, it should be to provide them with something meaningful that enhances your application, such as an academic, athletic, or cultural award that you have won, a new position that you have earned, or an essay or article that has been published, etc. Remember to keep your correspondence with a college at an appropriate level and do not badger them with too many letters, phone calls, or emails.

Keeping organized

If you have managed to write notes after every visit, you should now organize them and go through each one to evaluate your level of interest in each. You may have forgotten little details that you found appealing: the food in the cafeteria, the particular happy feeling you got from the students hanging out on the quad, or the renovated bathrooms in the dorms. Now is the time to bring those memories back and assess how important they are to you. The forms you used for your visit can also be used to keep track of any correspondence you had with the school and of all the material you sent. Keeping all this information in, say, one clear folder for each school, will keep you organized and on top of everything. The College Visit/Research sample template offers suggestions on aspects of the college to think about and record:

GETTING THROUGH IT TOGETHER

NAME OF SCHOOL (DATE OF VISIT/RESEARCH)   **MY LEVEL OF INTEREST IN THIS SCHOOL**

Admissions Regional Representative Name:
Phone: Email:

STUDENT POPULATION
Size: Undergraduates/Graduates:
Diversity: Temperament/'vibe': (friendly, quiet, serious, fun)
Academic atmosphere: relaxed, serious   School Spirit: sports, community involvement

COMMUNITY
Campus: Urban, Suburban, Rural   Campus: residential, spread out
Weather: First impressions:
Surrounding Neighborhood: 'Vibe', restaurants, shops, cinemas, parks/trees:

FACILITIES
Dorms: Singles, doubles, multiple, gender specific.   Condition of dorms:
Guaranteed dorm: Freshman Sophomore Junior Senior
Dining halls: Choice: Ambience: Payment type:
Athletic facilities: Fitness center, Pool:
Cultural activities: Theaters, Galleries, Libraries, etc:
Classrooms/labs/support facilities:

FINANCE
Tuition $ Accommodation $ Books $ Expenses$ Travel$
Scholarship opportunities:

ACADEMIC REQUIREMENTS
Average SAT score: Average ACT score: Average GPA:
Additional academic requirements: Years of High School instruction (Language, Social Studies)
                                SAT Subject tests:
Average class size: Popular majors/programs:
Availability of tutoring: Advisory support:
Career counseling/placement: Study abroad opportunities:

EXTRACURRICULAR ACTIVITIES
Greek Life: Athletics (club, intramural):   Community service:
Cultural events: Clubs: Other activities that interest you:

CONTACTS
Name:
Notes: (Position, department, notes, correspondence, etc.)

3.8 COLLEGE INTERVIEWS

Many colleges and universities interview students as part of their application process. It's an effective way for them to learn more about you beyond your application. Your interview will most likely be with someone from the admissions office, a current student, or a graduate of the college. It might take place at the school, at a nearby meeting place (like a coffee shop), or online through Skype or Face Time. Whatever form the interview takes, think of it as an opportunity to show that you are more than your grades. The most valuable thing you can when preparing for an interview is, well, to prepare. Here are some simple ways to prepare for a successful college interview:

Research the school
By knowing as much as possible about the school to which you are applying will give you a little extra confidence and make a favorable impression on your interviewer. Good places to start your research include:

- The college's website;
- Naviance – direct link to colleges through Scattergram, College Choice, and your college list;
- College guides (College Board, Fiske, Princeton Review, etc.);
- Online sites, such as Wikipedia, LinkedIn, etc.

To keep organized, compile information on each college. Template of questions, such as the one you used for your college visits, will be useful. Questions could include:

> College name;
> Location;
> Size of undergraduate population;
> Name of the department/school in which you are interested;
> Names of professors in particular fields of interest;
> Publications on research in your area of interest;
> Number of students in the department;
> Classes within the program in which you are interested.

If possible, learn about your interviewer
Having some knowledge of the person who will be interviewing you will be useful. Try to research one or two things about his/her accomplishments, history with the college, outside interests, and anything else that will help you break the ice. For information on your interviewer, you can search them by name on Google, LinkedIn, and perhaps even Wikipedia.

Think about what you want them to know about you
Before your interview, think about the three key qualities that you want to get across to the interviewer and be sure to bring them into the conversation. The interviewer will probably have seen your application and so knows your academic history. What he or she doesn't know is the special things that make you, you. Think about what strengths and/or characteristics might have got lost in the application. Are you exceptionally adventurous or creative? Are you a happy and optimistic person? Are you generous, kind, original, funny? Keep these traits in mind, and then weave them into your answers.

Have in mind some questions you want to ask
Your interviewer will appreciate your questions and may use them as an evaluation of your level of interest and commitment to the school. It is therefore important that you ask thoughtful questions: try not to ask questions that can easily be found on the website. Instead, think about questions that arise from issues that are important to you. For example, if you're seeking an active, engaged community, ask about participation rates in community service or recreational sports. Consider a question that requires an in-depth response, like "What type of student wouldn't fit in at this school?" or, "What aspect of campus are students working to improve?"

Practice, practice, practice!
Generally, interview questions fall into three main categories: Who are you? Where are you going? And, Why do you want this college? Questions – even the most casual of them – are geared towards getting a sense of your personality and an indication of how you would fit into the organization. If you're prepared to answer questions like these, you'll feel confident and have a positive interview experience. Go back over your reasons for wanting this school and practice the answers you will give to these questions. Be careful not to memorize answers though – you don't want to sound like a robot. Just be natural and listen careful to each question before you respond.

Be your best you
At your interview, be confident, relaxed, and respectful. Dress neatly. Be on time. And, above all, be yourself!

INTERVIEW MISTAKES AND HOW TO AVOID THEM

To many people interviews are like public speaking: nerve-wracking and something they would like to avoid at all costs. If you are nervous about interviews, there are some things to know that may help you alleviate those fears:

- Many interviewers are aware that the student they are interviewing may be nervous. They know that you have worked hard and that, if you are attending an interview, you really want to attend their college. They also understand that your desire to be admitted – and fear of not being admitted - could potentially affect your abilities to present yourself to your full advantage. Generally, college interviewers are skilled at asking questions that will encourage the student to speak comfortably about their studies and interests;

- Although there are many common mistakes, they are all avoidable. Below is a list of things that can go wrong with interviews and suggestions on how to avoid them and make the very best impression at every college interview.

Lack of Preparation
One of the most common mistakes that will virtually guarantee an unsuccessful interview is lack of preparation. One surprising example of this is when an interviewer asks a student something about an activity or experience they have written about in an essay, supplement, or list of extracurricular activities and the student can't remember what they wrote. Another question that can trip up the unprepared student is when an interviewer asks about the aspects of the college and/or major(s) that the student is particularly excited about. Finally, if you have expressed interest (or declared a major) in a particular subject or subjects, be prepared for questions relating to that subject or subjects. Your interviewer may be a teacher or professor and may ask in-depth questions.

How to avoid it: Although you might think that you can't prepare for an interview when you don't know what questions you will be asked, the examples above show that you actually can minimize the risk of not knowing how to answer questions:
- Re-read your application essay and supplements for the particular college. Think about what kind of questions you could be asked and write down some notes to help organize in your own mind some possible responses;
- If you referred to books or research by a professor at the college, re-read the material. Re-read the introduction to the book(s) and perhaps book reviews and recent critiques. Make notes on key points that a) you referred to and why you felt they were important, and 2) one or two opinions of others and a few notes on why you agree or disagree with them. With a professor's research, re-familiarize yourself with the exact research you mentioned and do additional reading about his/her publications, lectures, etc. to prepare yourself for possible academic discussion;
- Read through as much information as you can about the major and/or area of interest you indicated on your application. Make a note of the aspects of the course(s) that most interest you, and why;
- Keep an eye on news stories relating to your subject in case these should come up in conversation. Have an opinion on them, as this will show that you keep abreast of developments related to your subject;
- If you have expressed interest in studying English, prepare for questions, such as, "what are you reading at the moment?" and be reading something!

You cannot prepare for every question; in fact, interviewers may put questions to you because they know you will almost certainly not know the answer and they want to test your reactions within an unfamiliar experience, but you could certainly prepare for the basics and avoid embarrassing silences.

Relying on your achievements
A common mistake is to try and impress the interviewer with a list of your achievements. You have worked hard during your time at high school and it is only natural to want to show off a little. But, your interviewer will have seen your qualifications, grades, and awards on your application and will not need to hear you list them in person. The interviewer is interested in looking beyond these achievements to find out more about you: What motivates you, your opinions, and how you approach academic problems.
How to avoid it: If you are asked for your opinion on something, it is not enough to say that you have won an award in a related area – you need to demonstrate your intelligence by offering an opinion and engaging in academic discussion about it. This does not mean that you cannot mention your achievements; one way to do so in a non-boastful way would be to use an achievement as a springboard for discussing a particular skill. For example, if you were captain of the Robotics team (a fact on your application that the interviewer will most certainly have noticed), you could say, "Whilst competing at the global robotics championships in St. Louis, I really learned the importance of staying calm under pressure to keep the team motivated and on track."

Confusing courses, departments, even schools
If you have stated an 'area of interest' or declared a major, interviewers will expect you to be familiar with the area of study in which you have stated your interest on your application. It would be embarrassing (and, potentially, a disadvantage for you) if you confuse a course from another college with a course at this college. If you speak of your excitement to pursue the 'Global Peace' program, and no such program exists, it will be embarrassing for you. It is also advisable to avoid asking a question, such as, "what topics will I be studying?" You may think that this question shows the interviewer that you are showing interest but, actually, it indicates to the interviewer that you haven't sufficiently researched the program.

How to avoid it: Before you go into the interview, remind yourself about 1) the options you stated on your application for major/course/program/department/area, and 2) the content of the particular program, with a 'note to self' about certain classes that particularly appeal to you within that area of study.

Showing doubts
Displaying any kind of doubt about whether this is the college for you will get you crossed off the list immediately. It is also inadvisable to indicate in any way whatsoever that this college is anything but your first choice.
How to avoid it: Remain positive and enthusiastic at all times. You need to convince your interviewer that this college is your first choice and that it is the right place for you.

Dishonesty
Just as you should never lie in your application, essay, or personal statement, neither must you ever lie in an interview. One of the most common forms of dishonesty is a student telling an interviewer that they have read or done something to make themselves look more impressive, intelligent, or sophisticated.
How to avoid it: In a situation such as an interviewer asking if you have read a particular text and you haven't, it it is far better to be honest and say that you haven't read it YET, but that you have it on your list for your summer reading. If you have read other books by the same author, you could mention that and, if questioned about the book or the author's approach, offer your opinion. Don't be upset or anxious about not having read the book the interviewer initially asked you about. No interviewer will expect you to have read everything, and your honesty (and clever manipulation of the question to suit your area of knowledge) will be appreciated.

Being overly familiar
An interview is a formal situation and over-familiarity is not appropriate. However easy-going your interviewer seems to be, this is not the time to talk about personal matters.
How to avoid it: It is advisable on first meeting to greet your interviewer formally, using their title and surname. If the interviewer says, "Please call me (first name)", you can use their first name (but not overly often). This small informality, however, is a technique an interviewer might use to make you feel more comfortable, but it is not an invitation for you to tell him/her your life story and be overly familiar. A few pleasantries at the beginning and end of the interview are fine, but you should remain calm and professional at all times, and treat your interviewer with the utmost respect. Remember, as nice as the interviewer may seem (and probably is), he/she is there to do one thing: ascertain/judge if you are the right type of student for their academic institution.

Arrogance
Being invited to an interview is an indication that, on paper, you look good. It is not an admission and you still have a way to go before that decision is made. The interview is the college's one further component in the decision making process. A student who appears to assume that the college would be lucky to have them as a student and that their admission is guaranteed is going to come across as arrogant and potentially unpleasant.
How to avoid it: No matter how intelligent you are or how perfect you feel you would be at this educational institution, it is vital to remain professional and to put your opinions across respectfully. You can indicate that you feel or believe that you are suited to the college and give your reasons in a concise manner and modulated tone. During the interview, be aware of your body language; do not slouch, move too close to the interviewer, or lean back, all of which suggest that you may be too comfortable with the idea that you will be accepted.

Boredom
If you appear bored during the interview, the interviewer would certainly ask him/herself what you going to be like to teach. Apparent boredom can also be taken as a sign that you are not really interested in the college or in the area of study that you indicated in your application.
How to avoid it: You need to maintain enthusiasm and interest throughout the interview if you are to make a good impression. Even if you're not that interested in a particular topic of conversation, don't let it show. Keep focused on the conversation and don't allow your mind to drift.

Negativity
If you express negative opinions in the interview, you may be perceived as being a pessimistic or 'difficult' student and it may be the only thing that the interviewer remembers about you. Interviewers are looking for students with a positive attitude and outlook; negativity can be a disruptive force in a class and community and the interviewer may believe that your negative energy could bring down the mood of a class.
How to avoid it: It is important to adopt and maintain a positive and enthusiastic demeanor for the duration of the interview. Even if you feel yourself about to say something negative, you are better off not doing so – either don't say anything or turn it into a positive.

Body Language
Interviewers consider body language an important indicator of a person's personality and ability to cope under pressure. One of the most disconcerting body language traits is a person's inability to make eye contact. If a student can't make eye contact, they can appear timid and nervous, but they can also appear insincere and rude.
How to avoid it: The first thing to do is find out if you suffer from the trait of not making eye contact. You will need to ask the advice of friends, family, and/or teachers and they will hopefully be able to advise you if you are making an appropriate amount of eye contact.
In the interview, make a conscious and concerted effort to make frequent eye contact with your interviewer and, if there's more than one interviewer, look into the eyes of each one confidently from one to the other. If one of them asks you a question, maintain more eye contact with that person while you're answering their question.

Dressing inappropriately
Turning up to an interview dressed informally (think T-shirt, jeans, and trainers) is a big mistake. It indicates to the interviewer that you have not bothered to make an effort to make a favorable impression and that consequently, you do not show the appropriate level of respect for the institution to which you are applying.
How to avoid it: This is also an easy fix and one that instantly makes a good first impression. Always dress smartly for an interview and appreciate that 'smart' may have a different connotation in different schools and/or different regions. For example, some east coast schools tend to be more formal than those in, say, California or Oregon. Generally, an outfit comprised of smart pants and jacket for boys and a smart dress, or top and skirt combination for girls will work nationwide. With shoes, opt for smart shoes rather than trainers.

Being Late
Being late for an interview is surprisingly common. It is not always the student's fault, of course; traffic, weather, and any kind of transportation delay, can throw a curve ball in the best-laid plans. Sometimes though, it is just poor preparation and organization. Whatever the reason, it sets the wrong tone for the interview and does not look good for you.

How to avoid it: It may seem obvious, but lateness can be avoided simply by allowing far more time to get to the interview than you think you need. If you are traveling a long distance, you might consider going a day early and staying overnight. If you get stuck in unexpectedly severe traffic, or some other emergency befalls you on your journey, phone the college or department to let them know you're running late.

3.9 BUILDING YOUR COLLEGE 'BLUEPRINT'

One of the most useful resources for college information is the *College Handbook*, published by College Board. This enormous catalog includes information on every accredited college in the U.S. and is an extremely useful source to help you consolidate all the information you need on the schools you choose. There will no doubt be a copy or two in your counselor's office, the school library, and/or the local library. If is also available on Amazon. Make sure that you refer to the latest edition.

You can create your own list of colleges with relevant data in the Common Application and College Board websites, among others. It may sound old-fashioned, but a paper form of this information is really helpful: It is the central place for all the information you need on your college choices. You can pore over it, write notes on it, and, most importantly, have a visual reminder of what you're working for! The point is that if you tailor-make a list to your requirements (and cut and paste whenever a stage of the process is over or you don't need information any more) you have continual hard evidence that you are working towards something great. Information for each school generally includes the following information, but not necessarily all:

Type of school:
    Private, public, religious-affiliation, residential/commuter campus.
Size:
    Undergraduate and graduate student population by gender and ethnicity.
Admittance:
    Percentage of applicants admitted.
Graduation:
    Percentage of students who graduate within 6 years, sometimes percentage of students who enter graduate study.
General details:
    History, location, calendar type (semester/quarter), size of faculty, class size, and special facilities.
Freshman class profile:
    Number of admitted, and enrolled students in the past freshman class;
    Mid 50% scores on SAT components, and ACT;
    GPA, percentage of class with 3.75 and above; 3.50-3.74; 3.0-3.49; and 2.0-2.99;
    Class rank in top quarter and top tenth of their high school;
    Percentage return as sophomores;
    Percentage of out-of-state students;
    Percentage of students who live on campus;
    Percentage of international students;
    Percentage of students in fraternities and sororities.
Basis for selection:
    Most important factors of application used for admissions evaluation.
High School preparation:
    The minimum requirements for college application.

CHOOSING COLLEGES

Annual Costs:
Tuition fees, accommodation, books and supplies, and personal Expenses. These costs are the averages taken from across the entire student population. Costs are dependent on factors such as, course load, type of classes, accommodation, and lifestyle.

Financial Aid:
Information on need-based and non-need-based financial aid, scholarships/grants, loan average and number of students receiving aid.

Application Procedures:
Dates and submission types, application fee, deadlines for student application, scholarships, and financial aid applications.

Academics:
Information on special study options (combined, cross-registration, double majors, independent study, internships, study abroad, etc.)
Credit/placement by examination and/or advanced classes in high school
Support Services.

Majors:
Information on majors categorized into areas of study.

Most popular Majors:
Percentage of students within most popular majors.

Technology on campus:
Information on number of workstations, computers, internet access, online library, etc.

Student life:
Information on freshman orientation and preregistration, policies, housing, and activities.

Athletics:
Intercollegiate and intermural teams, team name(s). Sports for men or women only are indicated by (M) or (W). The athletic association to which the college belongs is indicated. Details of colleges belonging to NCAA (National Collegiate Athletic Association) and division levels are included in the index of the book, listed by sport. Other athletic associations indicated include:
- NAIA – The National Association of Intercollegiate Athletics. Members are mostly small colleges offering 13 sports.
- NJCAA – The National Junior College Athletic Association. Members are all two-year community or junior colleges.
- USCAA – United States Collegiate Athletic Association. Members are primarily very small colleges.
- NCCAA – National Christian College Athletic Association. Members are Bible colleges and other Christian-oriented institutions.

ROTC (The Reserve Officer Training Corps):
Indication of availability of ROTC program.

Student Services:
Counseling, employment, financial aid, graduate placement, learning support.

Contact information:
Names, addresses, email, phone, and fax numbers of college and relevant personnel.

You can build your college list based on the information that is important to you, in any format you choose. Below are examples of templates – the first with information on Ivy League schools and the second with information on a selection of California private and public schools:

Sample College Blueprint - Ivy League (information taken from College Board College Handbook, 55th edition)

College	% admit	Applied / admitted / enrolled	ACT/36	Basis for Selection	Most popular majors (%age)	Tuition $ p.a.
Brown	9	32,390 / 3,014 / 1,681	31-34	Strength of academic course load and student's achievement in courses most important; test scores strongly considered. Portfolio required for art, must programs. Alumni interviews available but not required for all applicants.	Biology 13, Computer/Information Sciences 6, Mathematics 6, Social Sciences 22, Visual/Performing Arts 6	51,366
Columbia	6	36292/ 2,279 / 1,420	32-35	Admission is highly selective using a holistic review process. Admission is not based on a simple formula of grades and test scores. Instead, a variety of factors are considered: academic record, extracurricular interests, intellectual achievements, and personal background.	Biology 10, Computer/Information Sciences 7, Engineering/Eng. Tech 21, Social Sciences 23	55,161
Cornell	14	44,965 / 6,337 / 3,315	31-34	HS achievement record (difficulty of courses, grades earned), test scores, preparation and background for specific programs especially important. Essays, recommendation, and extracurricular activities considered. Subject test requirements depend upon college/school. Interview required.	Agriculture 12, Biology 14, Business/Marketing 14, Computer/ Information Sciences 9, Engineering/Engin. Tech 16, Social Sciences 10	50,953
Dartmouth	11	20,675 / 2,190/ 1,121	31-34	Evidence of intellectual capability, motivation, and personal integrity of primary importance. Talent, accomplishment, and involvement in nonacademic areas also evaluated. Two SAT Subject tests of student's choice are recommended. Interview optional.	Biology 10, Engineering/Eng. Tech 8, History 6, Psychology 6, Social Sciences 35	51,438
Harvard	5	39,041 / 2,110 / 1,663	32-35	HS record most important; character, creative ability in some discipline or activity, leadership, liveliness of mind, demonstrated stamina and ability to carry out demanding college program, and strong sense of social responsibility important. Interview with alumnus/alumna required of all applicants if possible; documentation of special talent encouraged.	Biology 14, Computer/Information Sciences 6, History 8, Mathematics 11, Physical Sciences 7, Psychology 6, Social Sciences 30	47,074
Princeton	7	29,303 / 1,911 / 1,306	32-35	School achievement record and recommendations of guidance counselor and 2 teachers very important. 2 SAT subject tests, with certain requirements for different programs. Interview recommended when possible.	Biology 8, Engineering/ Engin. Tech 26, English 6, History 6, Physical Sciences 6, Psychology 6, Public Administrative/Social Services 12, Social Sciences 17	43,450
U Penn	9	38,918/ 3,674 / 2,491	32-35	Transcript indicating rigor of course work and achievement/evaluation most important criteria. Co-curricular involvements and testing strongly considered, as are counselor and faculty recommendations. Personal commentary (essays) and interview also considered. SAT Subject tests recommended. Entire SAT and ACT history to be submitted.	Biology 11, Business/Marketing 21, Engineering/Engin. Tech 9, Health Sciences 10, Social Sciences 16	53,534
Yale	6	31,445 / 1,988 / 1,371	32-35	Honors work at secondary level, test scores, and high degree of accomplishment in one or more nonacademic areas important, followed by diversity of interests, background, and special talents. SAT Subject tests recommended. Interview recommended.	Biology 10, Engineering/Engin. Tech 7, History 7, Interdisciplinary Studies 7, Psychology 6, Social Sciences 28	49,480

CHOOSING COLLEGES

Sample California College Blueprint (information taken from College Handbook by College Board, 55th edition)

College	U/Grad	Grad	% admit	GPA 3.75+	Rank top 1/4	SAT CR	SAT MA	ACT/36	Basis for Selection	Most popular majors (%age)
Stanford University	7,032	9,264	5	94	99	680-780	700-800	31-35	Academic excellence is primary criterion. Prospective students should have challenged themselves throughout high school and done very well. Transcript and recommendations are very important, as are personal qualities. SAT Sub tests recommended. AP exam scores recommended but not required.	Biology 6, Computer/Information Sciences 14, Engineering/Engineering Tech 23, Interdisciplinary Studies 17, Social Sciences 13
University California Berkeley	27,496	10,710	15	85	100	660-750	680-790	30-35	Thorough review of academic performance; likely contribution to intellectual and cultural vitality of the campus; diversity in personal background and experience; demonstrated qualities in leadership, motivation, concern for others and community, non-academic achievement in the performing arts, athletics, or employment; demonstrated interest in major. SAT subject tests recommended. GPA range 4.16-4.30	Biology 12, Engineering/Engineering Tech 12, Social Sciences 20
University California Irvine	27,331	5,423	41	87	100	500-630	560-700	N/i	Demonstrated record of academic preparation, educational engagement, talent and skills important. SAT Subject tests recommended but not required, but good scores may add positively to review of student's application.. Students need only submit scores for the ACT with Writing or SAT.	Biology 10, Business/Marketing 10, Engineering/Engineering Tech 10, Health Sciences 11, Psychology 12, Social Sciences 18, Visual/Performing Arts 6
University California Los Angeles	30,856	12,675	18	94	100	570-700	580-740	25-33	GPA, test scores, course work, number of and performance in honors and AP courses most important. Essay considered. Strong senior program important. Extracurricular activities, honors and awards also reviewed. SAT subject tests not required but reviewed if submitted; certain SAT subject tests may be recommended for some majors. SAT or ACT with writing examination is required.	Biology 13, Engineering/Engineering Tech 6, Interdisciplinary Studies 6, Mathematics 7, Psychology 10, Social Sciences 27
University California Santa Barbara	21,574	2,772	36	86	100	560-670	580-720	25-31	Eligibility established by HS GPA, course requirement, and SAT scores. SAT subject tests not required, but certain programs recommend them. Subject tests may satisfy some HS course requirements. College of Engineering recommends Math Level 2, College of Creative Studies recommends a SAT subject test related to student's major	Biology 9, Communications/Journalism 7, Interdisciplinary Studies 10, Psychology 8, Social Sciences 26
California Polytechnic San Luis Obsipo	20,367	697	29	75	88	560-660	590-700	26-31	Course work, HS GPA, test scores most important. Extracurricular activities considered.	Agriculture 13, Biology 6, Business/Marketing 12, Engineering/Engineering Tech 27, Parks/Recreation 6

When interpreting college data, the admission percentage rate of a college gives you and idea of where your GPA and test scores need to be to have a good chance of getting in. If the admittance rate of a school is at least 50%, and your GPA and test scores are about the same as the middle range for the freshman class, you can consider that a 'target school.' It is not guaranteed that you will be admitted, but the odds seem to be in your favor. If the acceptance rate of a school is between 25 to 45%, your grades and test scores would need to be near the high end of the range to consider that a target school. Any college that accepts fewer than 20% of the applicants is a highly selective school and usually a reach for anyone!

This is not an exact science and most colleges consider other factors, such as, activities, letters of recommendation, essays, and interview in the decision-making process. It's also important to remember the posted numbers include everyone who was admitted in the freshman class, including recruited athletes, legacy students, and students whose parents pay for buildings on campus. Those students don't necessarily have inferior qualifications, but it's fair to say that those in special interest groups have something colleges want, which sometimes makes grades and test scores less important.

<u>Narrowing down your list</u>
Another way to consider your college options is to ask yourself what is really important to you about each one on your list. On the following template you can grade each college according to different categories that you consider valuable. By totaling the 'scores' you will start to see which colleges emerge as favorites (if you don't already know):

Considerations for College Choices My interest - Ranking out of 10 (0 lowest to 10 highest)			
School Name	College A	College B	College C
Program focus			
Location			
Urban/Rural			
Campus			
Graduate prospects			
Size			
Greek Life			
Academics beyond major			
Social Life			
Languages			
Study abroad			
Status			
Sports			
Weather			
Proximity to home			
TOTAL			

Go the extra mile. It's never crowded.

− Unknown

3.10 PARENT POINTER - HELP WITH CHOOSING COLLEGES

When talking to your teen about college, it is helpful to think about the many considerations in choosing the right 'fit' college. What you consider an important consideration may not be so important to your teen, and vice versa. The table below offers ideas to get you all thinking – and talking:

\multicolumn{5}{c}{Considerations in choosing colleges}
Personality	**Skills**	**Aspirations**	**Experience**	**Other**
Enthusiasm	Academic skills	Focus of study	Academic/Social balance	Cost
Love of knowledge	Test scores	Career orientation	Location	Scholarships
Eagerness for college	GPA	Social consciousness	Size	Honors college
Independence	Extracurricular	Lifestyle	Safety	Legacy
Participant learning	Sports	Post graduation	Urban/Rural	Access to home
	Drama/Music/Art		Campus	Travel
			'Vibe	
			Greek life	
			Dorms / Food	

HELP WITH RESEARCHING SCHOOLS

Do not think that helping your teen at the choosing colleges stage is in any way 'interfering.' Many teens will not have the emotional energy or time to do all the legwork and research into colleges, especially if they have a heavy school workload and are doing a lot of extracurricular activities. You can help by talking about the considerations (above) and making notes on how important each is to them. For a first draft list, you can research schools that meet their criteria (even if their only criteria is location). Obviously, the more criteria you have, the better chance you have of building a more relevant first list. Once you have a list, encourage your teen to look them over with you and you can discuss them. Keep the conversation going and take seriously every comment they have. If your teen doesn't need help in this area and has already created a list of schools they like, ask them questions about their choices. Other things you can do to help are:

- Attend the high school information sessions: on the college search process, financial aid, and other topics;
- Attend college events (such as college fairs and college presentations), BUT let your teen lead the charge: Be careful not to ask all the questions or be over friendly with the college reps in your quest to get your teen noticed and remembered;
- Encourage visiting a College Fair. If your teen is showing resistance to attending the fair (or college in general), you could ask them if they would like to arrange a few friends to go along at the same time. It might mean them saying that they would rather you not join them, but don't take it personally. Your teen may be ready to take some control of his or her own destiny;
- Get access to The College Handbook by College Board includes information on every accredited college in the U.S. From this book, I suggest students build a College Blueprint with the information that is immediately relevant to them (e.g. GPA, standardized test scores, GPA, and most popular majors). Together you can add to the blueprint relevant information to your family, such as tuition fees and expenses. Later, you can add other relevant information, e.g., applications fees and deadlines (see example templates), such as in the example below:

GETTING THROUGH IT TOGETHER

College	U/Grad	% admit	ACT	HS preparation recommendations/requirements	Basis for Selection	Cost $ Tuition	Living	Books	Exps
Brown University, Providence, RI	6,580	9	31-34	College prep program recommended. 16 units required, 21 recommended. Required and recommended units include English 4, Math 4, SS 1, History 2, Science 3-4 (lab 2-3), FL 3-4, Vis/PA 1, academic electives 1. Future Science, Math, engineering students will benefit from more advanced courses in those areas.	Strength of academic course load and student's achievement in courses most important; test scores strongly considered. Portfolio required for art, must programs. Alumni interviews available but not required for all applicants.	51,366	13,200	1,540	2,000
Vassar College, NY	2,401	27	30-33	College prep program recommended. 20 units recommended. Recommended units include English 4, Math 4, SS 2, History 2, Science 3 (lab 3), FL 4. Advanced and accelerated courses recommended whenever possible. Minimum of 20 units recommended with additional unit in Science, foreign language, and social studies.	Academic credentials most important. Personal achievements, essay, and recommendations also carefully considered. Evidence that students have elected most demanding program available crucial. 2 SAT subject tests of student's choice required.	53,090	12,400	900	1,350
Fordham NY	9,096	45	27-31	College prep program required. 15 units required; 20 recommended. Required and recommended units include English 4, Math 3-4, SS 3-4, Science 3-4, FL 2-4.	HS achievement record most important, followed by test scores, class rank, extracurricular activities, recommendations, and essay. Personal characteristics, special talents and relationship to Fordham University also considered.	49,073	16,845	1,012	1,814
George Washington, DC	11,244	40	27-32	College prep program required. Required and recommended units include English 4, Math 2-4, SS 2-4, Science 2-4 (lab 1), FL 2-4. 1 Physics, 1 chemistry, and additional 1 unit in Math required for School of Engineering and Applied Science.	Strong college prep program, 3.0 GPA and class rank in top third important. Teacher and counselor recommendations and personal statement required. SAT subject tests required for applicant to 7-year BA/MD and integrated engineering/MD programs (any Math and any Science) and recommended for all for admission and placement. Interview recommended for all, required of early admission applicants.	51,950	12,500	1,275	1,500
NYU	25,716	32	29-33	16 units required: 20 recommended. Required and recommended units including English 4 Math 3-4, SS 3-4, history 3-4, Science 3-4 (lab 3-4), FL 3-4	HS achievement record most important. Test scores, activities, essays, recommendations also important. NYU has flexible testing policy.	49,062	17,578	1,070	2,000
UC Berkeley	27,496	15	30-35	College prep program required. 15 units required: 18 recommended. Required and recommended units include English 4, Math 3-4, History 2, Science 2-3 (lab 2-3), FL 2 -3, Vis/PA 1, academic electives 1. 2 units in history or social Sciences are required.	Thorough review of academic performance; likely contribution to intellectual and cultural vitality of the campus; diversity in personal background and experience; demonstrated qualities in leadership, motivation, concern for others and community, non-academic achievement in the performing arts, athletics, or employment; demonstrated interest in major. SAT subject tests recommended. GPA range 4.16-4.30	13,485 / 40,167 (out of state)	15,562	1,240	4,598

(SS - Social Science, FL - Foreign Language, Lab - laboratory, Vis/PA - Visual Performing Arts)

FINANCES

For many families, financing college is a major consideration. It is important therefore, that you talk to your teen about the financial situation regarding their college choices. Private colleges can be very generous and merit scholarships are often determined automatically on application. With funding, private colleges may therefore be as competitive price-wise as public colleges.

CONVERSATIONS ABOUT COLLEGES

As a parent, it might be frustrating to hear your teen suggest a college that you 'know' to be clearly unsuitable for them. It is important not to immediately dismiss their suggestion, but to ask them why they are attracted to that college. Maybe this particular college is the one everyone is talking about at school. Your teen may be 'socializing' the idea of it with you, not necessarily because it is a college they particularly like – or even know much about - but perhaps for other reasons, such as:

- *Saying it aloud makes college – any college – a reality to them;*
- *They admire the people who say they are applying to this particular college;*
- *They feel more mature by showing that they are thinking about their future;*
- *They want your opinion.*

It is wise to ask questions about their choices rather than immediately giving them your opinion. Questions to get your teen thinking might include:

- *Is there something particular about the college that interests you?*
- *Do you know of anyone else looking at the college? And, if so, what do you think they like about it?*
- *Does it have most of the things that are important to you? (E.g., location, size, major, Greek life, etc.)?*

When offering an opinion, try to avoid saying things like, how 'easy' it was to get into that college when you were a student or that you know it to be a 'party school', or that it doesn't have a good reputation for this or that major. Your teen may be offended and/or embarrassed and may find it difficult in future conversations to tell you the colleges they are thinking about. Constructive ways to offer your opinion could be:

- *If your teen doesn't seem to know much about the college – and neither do you - suggest that you research it together and see if it has all (or some) of the criteria they consider important;*
- *If you know about the college and consider it in some way inappropriate for your teen, offer your opinion in a way that indicates to them that you are being open minded. You could start your opinion with opening statements such as:*

    - *"I don't know if this is true, but I heard from a colleague that this college has a reputation for ……."*
    - *"I was surprised to learn that the college lacks ………";*
    - *" I don't know much about this college, but I read an article recently ……."*
    - *"I've heard of this college and understand that it has an excellent……….program, but I'm not sure that it offers exactly what you are looking for."*

MANAGING EXPECTATIONS
It is important to manage both your and your child's expectations when looking at colleges. Once a college list is made 'public' to family and friends, it can take on a life of its own and becomes, inadvertently, an indicator of the student's capabilities. The list situates the student on an instantly recognizable matrix: If the student's list consists of Princeton, Dartmouth and Vanderbilt, for example, most people will surmise that the student is bright and would undoubtedly have good grades and test scores. Conversely, if a student's list consists of lesser-known colleges, the opposite assumptions may be made. Your teen does not need that pressure or negativity.

High achieving students may start talking about colleges that are extremely competitive. It is commendable that these teens are aiming high and working hard for their dreams, but it is really important that you help them manage their expectations. In the initial phases of the college conversations, your teen may like to hear him or herself saying out aloud the names of colleges that everyone has heard of and are known to be notoriously competitive. If you and/or your teen are talking about colleges with less than a 20% admittance rate, it is advisable to:

- Create a college blueprint as soon as possible. Detail the admittance information so that your teen can see at a glance the criteria for these colleges (see the section on building a college list);
- Look over your teen's transcript with them and compare their qualifications so far (e.g., GPA, class rank, AP and Honors classes, extracurricular activities, etc.) against the criteria of each college.
- If your teen has a particular major in mind, suggest that they research colleges that have a strong program in that field;
- Help balance the 'big name' colleges with more accessible schools and suggest a 50-50 split in the college list, i.e. a college with an admittance rate of, say, 40% and above, to every college with less than 20% admittance rate;
- The big name colleges are academic. They expect in their applicants demonstration of academic intensity, interest, success, and potential. It is a good idea to discuss with your teen the level of academic challenge they want to take on. It is one thing telling people you are going to apply to a highly selective college, another thing to actually be admitted, and yet another to keep up with the challenge and workload. Being realistic about college choices in the early stages will help keep your teen grounded and save them potential heartache and embarrassment in the future.

Managing expectations early on in the process will help your teen realize that there are many more colleges out there than those that everyone knows or talks about. With a large range of colleges to consider – including those that are a great 'fit' for them – your teen will feel more in control of the process and will not consider him or herself a 'failure' if they do not get into the big name college.

Children learn more from what you are than what you teach.

- W.E.B DuBois

CHAPTER 4

COLLEGE APPLICATIONS

If you tell the truth you don't have to remember anything.

― Mark Twain

4.1   TYPES OF COLLEGE APPLICATIONS

THE COMMON APPLICATION

The Common Application - referred to most often as the 'Common App' - is the most widely used college application with membership of over 800 academic institutions in the U.S. and overseas. Almost all of those member colleges and universities use the Common App exclusively and most will also have an individual supplement (with additional questions and essay prompts) that must be completed. The Common App allows students to apply to a maximum of 20 colleges and is a vehicle for the collecting, collating, and distributing supplementary student materials to its member institutions throughout the application process. The Common App is free to use, but virtually all member institutions charge an application fee to applicants, ranging from $25 - $90. The newly designed format for the 2019-20 applications cycle contains information, tips, videos, and responses to frequently asked questions (www.commonapp.org).

THE COALITION APPLICATION

The Coalition Application for Access, Affordability, and Success, launched in 2016, is a central applications platform for member colleges and universities. It is similar to the Common Application in that universities and colleges can become member schools, and those members use the platform to collect and collate applications, transcripts, letters of recommendation, and essays. Also like the Common App, schools can attach their individual requirements (additional information and supplemental writing) to the main application. The Coalition Application includes top colleges and universities (including the Ivy League), many of which also use the Common Application (www.coalitionforcollegeaccess.org).

THE UNIVERSAL APPLICATION

The Universal Application is used by about 50 colleges, some of which also accept the Common Application, e.g. Harvard and Cornell. The colleges treat them as equal vehicles for application and do not favor one over the other (www.uca.applywithus.com).

PUBLIC STATE SCHOOLS and INDEPENDENT APPLICATIONS

Public state schools, such as the University of California, typically have their own application systems. The generic information requirements are similar on all applications, but essay and supplementary writing requirements vary from system to system. For example, the University of California application requires four essays (www.universityofcalifornia.edu) and the California State University system does not require any (www2.calstate.edu).

HANDLING THE APPLICATIONS

All applications have a similar format: they all require generic personal information and academic information. Most require details on extracurricular activities and an indication of preferred academic area. Most also require some form of writing in the form of essays, personal statements and/or statements of major and/or college choice. Remember to read each question carefully and provide all information required. All of the applications sites provide excellent guidelines on how to complete them. The Common Application has more member colleges than any other applications service, and it is most likely that at least one of your chosen colleges will use it, so it is used here as the guideline for completion.

4.2 COMPLETING THE COMMON APPLICATION

Open up your applications as soon as they are available and start to fill in requirements for generic data first. It will be helpful to have your résumé and transcripts easily accessible so that you can complete the necessary formalities in one sitting. The essays and supplements are going to take more time.

4.2.1 Generic Information

- Use the same name on everything. Even though there is a box for a "preferred nickname" and even if you complete it, continue to use your proper name throughout the application;
- Put your name and either your address or your Social Security number on everything you submit;
- When completing the Family section, check details, such as their career titles, education, and graduation dates with your family;
- If you state an area of academic interest, make sure that it exists at the college to which you are applying;
- Make sure you respond to the question on whether or not you require financial aid;
- List your best SAT and/or ACT scores and the dates taken. Unless specifically required, you do not need to include a test in which you have not received any higher score than in others (i.e., it will not be used for super scoring);
- List all awards or distinctions from 9th grade onwards;
- In the Activities section, indicate your most important activities first and the years involved. You should be concise in your description of your participation and be honest about the hours per week you spend doing an activity. If you would like to expand on a particular activity, you can use the 'Additional Information' section, but only if you feel it is absolutely relevant and appropriate. Perhaps consult your counselor for guidance on this. See section 4.2.2 below for examples on how to make the most of your activities;
- Do not repeat in your essays information that you have supplied in the Activities section. You may tell a story about the activity, but only if it tells the admissions officers something that does not appear elsewhere on your application.

The 'Writing' section of the Common App is where the Common App essay prompts reside. See Chapter 5 for guidance on writing the essays and supplements.

4.2.2 Presenting Activities

Like every aspect of the application, the Activities list is an important part of the overall picture or 'narrative' of you as a person and student. It is advisable to spend time thinking carefully about this section. Along with the essay, activities provide insight into your personality beyond the classroom. Following are some tips to keep you focused and organized:

- List activities according to importance to you and years involved;
- Describe activities such as community service or robotics, but under no circumstances should you list shopping or video gaming as extracurricular activities;
- There are only 32 weeks in a school year, so beware of overstating your hours or time commitment;

- With only 150 characters in the description box, you must be judicious with your words and not repeat anything. If you describe your role in the top box, you do not need to repeat it in the description box. For example:

    Weak: (top box) School newspaper
    (description box) I am the editor for the school newspaper

    Specific: (top box) Editor of International Column, School Newspaper
    (description box) Responsible for brainstorming, revising, and supervising articles by other writers for my column.

You should maximize the value of your activities in the description box by being SPECIFIC, such as in the examples below:

1. Be specific and emphasize achievements

    Weak: Raised money for children in Africa.
    Strong: Raised $2,580 to buy two wheelchairs for hospital in Kenya through Aid Africa USA project

2. Explain using active verbs

    Weak: Worked at a clinic doing a variety of different things.
    Strong: Organized patient diagnosis notes, sterilized tools for surgeries, assisted with x-ray analysis.

3. Cut out unnecessary words. Put activities in list form and use dynamic words (underlined)

    Weak: I raised money to donate to a school in Nepal by collecting bread tags.
    Strong: Raised $1,800 for school in Nepal: Led advertising campaign, organized fundraisers, presented results to regional committee.

4. Use the present tense if you continue to do the activity

    Weak: I took visitors around the campus and gave them information on school history and student life.
    Strong: Organize campus tours, guide prospective students and parents, answer questions, present mission statement, introduce principal and counselors.

5. Aim for variety in your list. Do not use any redundant words or repeat verbs

    Weak: Instructing, helping, and teaching children soccer (these verbs all mean the same)
    Strong: Coach, children's soccer camp: instruct on technique, teach sportsmanship, advice on good health.

6. Include any responsibilities where you had to demonstrate leadership skills

    Weak: I swim on the swim team.
    Strong: Lead swim practices, assist coach in scheduling, arrange food and transportation for meets.

7. Include any responsibilities you have or had that demonstrate leadership skills and use dynamic words

    Weak: I helped arrange marketing, and showed results to class.
    Strong: <u>Responsible</u> for <u>brainstorming</u> ideas for marketing campaign, <u>presenting</u> results to school, and <u>promoting</u> fundraising activities.
    (Note: even if you were not the leader of the campaign, you can show how you were involved at specific levels of the activity).

4.2.3 College Application Tips

- If everyone in your class is talking about a particular college, it is likely that they are planning to apply, potentially reducing your chances of admission. If there's a school you want to attend, keep it to yourself!
- Colleges give 'points' for geographical diversity (state and rural/urban), ethnicity, athletic abilities, special talents, and legacy (having family members who attended the school). Ensure that you indicate in your application any of your particular circumstances, qualities, and attributes;
- If you don't need financial aid, let the colleges know. If the school is short on funds or loaded with applicants who need aid, they will want some full fee-paying students;
- If you want to let the colleges know you are really interested, ask for an interview with the admissions officer and talk to the professors in your desired major. You'll stand out as an applicant;
- A college is more likely to accept you if your major is in an 'under-enrolled' area. Ask the admissions officer how your choice of major might affect your chances;
- Stand out! Colleges give extra points for talent and athletic ability. Let them know what you can do;
- Take control of your own destiny. Do not let your parents make phones calls to the college for information. You may not be as polished on the telephone as your parents, but admissions officers will note that *you* made the contact and will appreciate your enthusiasm and interest;
- Make sure you have a 'balanced' college list and don't apply to only 'reach' colleges. You must have some more accessible colleges on your list and you must give those colleges just as much care and attention in your applications;
- Market yourself! If you have a special talent, such as art, photography, music, etc. - send a sample of your work. Many colleges now accept submissions through Slideroom or ZeeMee for such additional material;
- If you feel that you are unable to put across details about yourself and your life within the parameters of the application essay, you can submit added information or explanations. Make sure your social security number and name is on every page;
- Call every college you've applied to and make sure your application has been received and is complete. If anything is missing, get it to them quickly;
- Send thank you notes after interviews, visits, or if an admissions officer has been particularly helpful. You'll get your name in front of them again;
- If you didn't get an offer from your favorite college, perhaps consider transfer at a later stage. Community college can be an attractive (and cost effective) solution to (eventually) getting into the college of your dreams. Find out what your favorite colleges uses as its 'feeder' school and do your 2-year core curriculum there. Depending on colleges, there may also be a guaranteed transfer program, so make sure you find out about that too;

- Apply Early Decision only to your first choice college. Apply Early Action to as many colleges as allow. You will receive responses earlier than in Regular Decision submissions;
- If you know alumni from the college - a relative, employer, volunteer supervisor - ask them to write a letter of recommendation for you.

4.3 EVALUATION OF APPLICATIONS

College applications are an in-depth record of a student's academic qualifications, extracurricular activities, and special skills and qualities. College applications contain templates into which the student completes the complete scope of information relating to his or her academic life, in the following categories:

Proven Academic Performance
Your transcript of courses and grades for all your years in high school is the single most important part of the application. It reflects academic ability, interests, and achievements over time. Through that information, a college admissions officer can determine rigor, depth, and performance. Institutions consider at least the final three years of high school and look for students who have taken challenging classes. It is therefore important to take the most demanding classes appropriate for you.

Standardized Testing
Your SAT or ACT scores are recognized by many institutions as reliable predictors of success during your first year of college. SAT Subject Test scores are also considered valuable predictors of performance. Most selective institutions require scores from the SAT or ACT and require or 'recommend' scores from two or three different SAT Subject Tests. Many schools do not require the SAT Subject test scores, but will consider them if submitted. However, generally, most schools require them of home-schooled students. It is important that you research the specific requirements for institutions in which you are interested.

Activities
Activities demonstrate to the college admissions officers the commitment you have to activities beyond academics; be it sports, community and volunteer work, drama, or other interests. Remember though, it is much more important to show depth and longevity in one activity than it is to show marginal involvement in broad array of activities.

Teacher Recommendations
Most colleges require two teacher recommendations. College admissions offers use teachers' comments to evaluate a student's potential as a college student. Some applications (such as the Common Application) have a somewhat free format teacher evaluation, allowing teachers to answer questions in their own words. This kind of format includes questions, such as:

- In what subject did you teach this student?
- How long have you known this student, and in what context?
- What are the first words that come to mind to describe this student?
- In which grades was the student enrolled when you taught him/her?
- List the courses in which you have taught this student, including the level of course difficulty (AP, IB, accelerated honors, electives, 100-level, 200-level, etc.);
- Additional comments.
- Teachers may also use the rating format, similar to the one used by counselors (see letters of recommendation section in Chapter 2).

Character

College admission officers also take into account your character and personal qualities. Colleges are most interested in what makes you unique and how you will contribute to the college community and they look for these qualities in your application:

- Leadership
- A willingness to take risks
- Initiative
- A sense of social responsibility
- A commitment to service
- Special talents or abilities

Overall, colleges want a mix of students to create a rich campus community: they look for students who are more than their grades, who like to get involved in activities, who demonstrate curiosity and enthusiasm, and who indicate that they are going to contribute just as much, if not more, than they gain from the college experience. Evidence of these attributes are found in a student's demonstration of:

Extracurricular Activities

What you do outside the classroom reveals a lot about you. That is why most applications ask for details about extracurricular activities. But remember, it's not the number of activities that's important. Admission officers want to know what you've learned and how you've grown from participating in these activities. Unless an application specifies which order to state your activities, you should rank them by importance to you. Also, do not 'pad out' your list with activities that you did a long time ago or are insignificant. This same rule applies to the estimation of hours involved: be careful to be honest and realistic.

Athletics

A "recruited" athlete is a student who has been contacted by a coach. It is important that a prospective college athlete keep their college adviser in the communication loop at all times. Information relating to recruited athletes and their responsibilities is available through the NCAA (National College Athletic Association) and you should pay close attention to all information from the recruitment coach, your school coach, and your college adviser. Generally, the activities you should consider doing during the summer of your junior year include registering with the NCAA Initial-Eligibility Center.

The NCAA Eligibility Center was established for athletic eligibility and certification purposes. If you hope to be recruited by a Division I or Division II school and take an expense-paid visit to their campus (whether it be a meal, an arranged over-night accommodation, and/or travel expenses), you must register and be certified for initial eligibility by the Eligibility Center prior to your visit. These visits generally take place in your senior year. This criteria applies to expense-paid visits. You may visit any campus at any time at your own expense for academic purposes.

You can register with Eligibility Center online at: https://web3.ncaa.org/ecwr3/ and complete forms to release transcripts before the end of junior year. You must also send test scores to the NCAA Eligibility Center. A credit card is needed to pay your registration fee. Once you are registered, you should contact your high school counselor and ensure that your transcripts are sent, usually by the end of June. Mailing address is:

>   NCAA Eligibility Center
>   Certification Processing
>   P O Box 7136
>   Indianapolis, IN 46207
>   Tel: 877-262-1492 (toll free).

Visual and Performing Arts
For the student who has done a significant amount of visual artwork, music, dance, or theater and who intends to pursue one of these fields in college, it is recommended that you create a portfolio or DVD of your best work. Plan well ahead, particularly if you plan to ask a teacher for assistance or a Letter of Recommendation to accompany the piece. You should follow the guidelines indicated by each individual college on its website.

Summer Jobs and Activities
Your summer experiences also provide insight into your character. Having a summer job at a fast-food restaurant can build as much character as attending a prestigious summer learning program. For college admissions officers, it is about what you have gained from the experience, what you have learned, and how you communicate those in your applications. Remember to be specific and enthusiastic.

The Essay(s) and Supplementary Writing
The essay and supplementary writing give you the opportunity to show the admission officers who you are and how you will contribute to the college campus. They can reveal your character in ways that your qualifications cannot. It is important to take your time to write the very best essays and supplements you can. For guidance on writing, see Chapter 5.

Letters of Recommendation
Letters of Recommendation can reveal a lot about the kind of person you are. When reading your letters of recommendation, college admissions officers look for evidence of personal qualities, such as leadership, curiosity, work ethic, and respect. A teacher who has seen you work hard to master difficult material and earn high grades will very likely indicate on his or her letter of recommendation your qualities such as your work ethic, determination, and intellectual curiosity. A counselor who sees you helping freshman acclimatize to their new school will indicate personal attributes associated with such an activity, such as your kindness, leadership abilities, and dedication to school and community.

Be aware that some colleges are very strict on the number of letters of recommendation required and will not accept more than the stated number. Some, however, welcome additional letters, particularly if they pertain to explain circumstances that have not been able to be explained elsewhere, such as a drop in grades, move to another school, etc.

Special Talents
Colleges want a well-balanced student body, and this means that they look for students with specific talents. Let them know if you have something different or special to contribute to the college community. If you have a poem published in a high school journal or book, if you have had your artwork displayed in a public place, or if you play guitar with a local folk band, let the college admissions people know. Having good grades and being a good person are expected of everyone and, therefore, if you have some additional quality, make sure you indicate it on your application.

Evidence of Leadership
Leadership comes in many forms and colleges are interested in students who demonstrate leadership abilities in any areas of their lives. Leadership abilities may appear to be most obvious in students in positions such as, captain of the football team or president of the student council, and there will be due consideration given to students who have the leadership qualities required for such roles. If you have not held such obvious leadership roles, it is important to elaborate on other ways in which you have been able to lead and to demonstrate that you are comfortable with it. Leading a project or activity, tutoring peers or younger

students, being a mentor or 'buddy' to incoming freshmen, or taking care of family members and commitments are all indications that you have a level of comfort with some form of leadership.

Proven leadership abilities are highly valued in college admissions. Thousands of students have excellent grades and test scores, but what often sets an applicant apart is his or her involvement in school clubs, athletics, or community organizations and, particularly, in a leadership role of some form. Working their way through an activity and gaining the respect of others to earn a leadership position is especially attractive to college admissions officers, showing them that you have commitment, dedication, character, and an excellent work ethic. Leadership comes in a variety of forms and in a variety of activities, which include:

- Student Government, Student Council;
- Academic teams - math team, debate club, etc.;
- Arts - theater, band, choir, dance, etc.;
- Athletic teams;
- High school clubs and organizations;
- Fund-raising activities;
- Community service and volunteering;
- Employment - after school jobs, internships, etc.;
- Peer tutoring;
- Political organizations - Model U.N., International Relations Club, etc.;
- Publications - school newspaper, literary magazine, yearbook, etc.;
- School 'Ambassador' role.

A significant leadership role or two can make the difference between a good application and an excellent one. The National Honor Society characterizes student leaders as:

> "Resourceful, good problem solvers, promoters of school activities, idea-contributors, dependable, and persons who exemplify positive attitudes about life."

Being a leader shows college admissions officers that you are a persona of character and that you are well qualified to enter college and thrive. Suggestions of how you can explore leadership positions include:

Know your Strengths
People always talk about 'passions' – finding them, following them – and this can be very frustrating when you don't feel passionate about anything. If that is the case, forget passion and think, simply, about what you like doing or what makes you happy. If you are a 'people person' and like to be in the midst of all the action, think about student government or becoming a school ambassador or buddy for the incoming freshman class. If you like to write or have an interest in photography, join the school newspaper or yearbook. If you love history and want to get others interested, start a club – say, a History and Film club where you get together to watch a movie related to a particular historical period followed by a discussion session. To become a leader, consider the following:

<u>Gain Experience</u>
Accept the fact that you will probably not be a leader straight away. Work to achieve that goal. If you work as a reporter or photographer on the school newspaper in freshman and sophomore year, and have consistently shown your interest and commitment, you have a good chance of a leadership position in Junior and Senior year. If drama is your thing and you haven't yet had the chance to be in a leading role,

do your very best in the parts you are given, show up to every rehearsal, and work on your technique: your time will come.

Work with Others
A key characteristic of good leaders is their inter-personal skills. To be a good leader is to treat people with respect, listen to them, ask questions, and establish trust. Be inclusive and work to create a sense of teamwork.

Be Optimistic
A positive attitude is a key component of good leadership. Believe in yourself and others, especially when faced with difficult or challenging circumstances.

Be a Good Sport
For the athletic leader particularly, it is important to show good sportsmanship. Grace, good manners, and positivity are highly commendable qualities in any leader; in sports, they are especially valuable when tensions run high and there is always a win-lose scenario.

Live with Integrity
Good leaders set goals and follow the steps necessary to achieve them. People look up to them because they are visionary, loyal, and dependable and they live their lives with integrity; that is they are honest, reliable, and honorable. Whatever leadership position you have in whatever field you choose, integrity will always be your most valuable asset.

Actions are More Important than Titles
Leadership comes in all sorts of forms. Even if you do not become Editor-in-Chief of the school newspaper, you can still make outstanding contributions through well-written articles, well-researched stories, or memorable photographs. Even if you are not captain of the soccer team, you can be a solid team player, showing up for every conditioning and practice and giving your 'all' in every game. Your contribution, commitment, and achievement are far more important than your title. If you have made an exceptional contribution to an activity, ask your coach, mentor, teacher, or leader, to write a letter of recommendation, which you can send in with your college application materials if permitted.

4.3.1 FERPA – The Family Educational Rights and Privacy Act

FERPA is a federal law that protects the privacy of student education records. The law applies to all schools that receive funds under an applicable program of the U.S. Department of Education. FERPA gives parents certain rights with respect to their children's education records. These rights transfer to the student when he or she reaches the age of 18 or attends a school beyond the high school level. Students to whom the rights have transferred are referred to as "eligible students."

There is a section on the Common Application and other applications that gives a student the option to waive their rights to view the entire contents of their college application, which specifically relates to letters of recommendation from teachers and your college counselor. You should consider waiving your rights because doing so suggests that the recommendations have been written objectively. You should be aware that if you do not waive your rights to access your documents, there is the potential for college admissions officers to see it as a 'red flag' and question why you need to see your documents and they will perhaps want to investigate, for example, whether you have been in trouble or you are a difficult student. When you do not waive your rights, you may, upon attending that institution, have access to the

COLLEGE APPLICATIONS

full contents of your college application, including recommendations. However, you do not have access to applications to colleges that you do not attend.

4.4 FINANCIAL AID

A key piece of the college applications process for many families centers on financial aid. Outlined below are explanations of the steps in applying for aid, how colleges factor financial aid into admissions and award packages, and how the typical financial aid package might be developed. Policies vary from college to college and it is therefore essential that you refer to the specific requirements of each college. It is also advisable to call the colleges direct if you have questions.

When applying for financial aid, each college will have specific requirements for financial aid, so it is important that you read the information on each application and fill out the required forms, one of which will be the **FAFSA (Free Application for Federal Student Aid)**. All students applying for any federal financial aid must file a form as soon as possible after January 1st of the application year. Analysis of the data on this form will determine eligibility for Federal Pell Grants, Supplemental Educational Opportunity Grants (SEOG), Federal Work Study, Stafford Loans (subsidized and unsubsidized), and other federal and state programs. Many states, while often requiring their own forms, will also require the FAFSA to award state grants to students. Since federal aid is a key component of most awards, it is critical that this is filed in a timely manner. You can file the FAFSA free of charge online at www.fafsa.ed.gov.

Separate from the FAFSA is the **CSS Profile (College Scholarship Service),** which many private colleges require to help determine a student's eligibility for the institution's own funds. The CSS Profile is available exclusively online at www.collegeboard.org, and is typically due by the same date as the student's application.

In addition to the CSS Profile, families may be asked to submit, if applicable, a Non Custodial Parent (NCP) application. Students applying to colleges that required the NCP will be given information about the process after they have registered for the Profile and will be asked to pass the instructions to their noncustodial parent. Some schools may also require additional information on their own Institutional Form, as well as copies of tax returns to verify information.

If a family cannot afford to pay for four years of college without assistance from outside resources, you should apply for financial aid. In order that you are clear about a school's policies, and to help you make informed decisions about where to apply, ask any or all of the following questions of the admissions office or when visiting schools:

- Does the college practice a need-blind admissions policy?
- What percentage of students receives financial aid?
- What percentage of students have their full need met?
- What percentage of the funds was need-based?
- What percentage of the funds (if any) was merit based?
- Do the same financial aid procedures and policies apply for all four years?
- If my family has more than one student in college, will that be taken into consideration when calculating my family contribution?
- If the cost of college toes up, will my aid go up accordingly?
- Can the school's financial aid be used to cover the costs of study abroad programs?

- How are outside scholarships handled? Are they credited against the loan component of my aid, the grant component, or the family contribution?
- Do I need a certain GPA (Grade Point Average) to keep my merit grant?
- Are emergency funds available for short-term loans?
- Are there are tuition payment plans that will allow my parents and I to spread out our payments?
- What is the policy with regard to non-custodial parents and stepparents? Are they expected to contribute if financially able?
- What is the typical financial aid package?
- How much debt can I expect after four years?
- How many hours a week will I have to work to fulfill the work-study portion of my aid package?

Every college should have some form of a financial aid calculator on its website. This form is used to calculate the Expected Family Contribution (EFC) and financial need, and to estimate your student financial aid. This free service will give you a sense of what you might qualify for in terms of grants, loans, and scholarships. Colleges do not retain any record of the information you submit on this form. (www.finaid.org). College Board also has its own version of a calculator and contains other tips on how to pay for college (www.collegeboard.org).

The **Expected Family Contribution (EFC)** is determined after income and assets are reviewed. Allowances are made for the number of family members, the number of children in college, necessary expenses, etc. Generally, you are asked to contribute a portion of your personal savings and other assets. You are also expected to contribute a certain amount based on what you could realistically earn during the summer, whether or not you choose to work. Should you receive merit-based awards from organizations outside of the college, these are considered as part of your available resources and may be applied against the self-help portion of your aid package. Consideration is also given to special financial circumstances (illness, older parents approaching retirement, or special educational needs). Be certain that colleges are aware of any unusual circumstances that may exist in your family.

You should also be aware that colleges handle family situations differently in cases where parents are separated, divorced, and/or remarried. Some colleges take into consideration the income and assets of the stepparent with whom the student lives, whilst others do not. Federal fund eligibility (determined by FAFSA) is based on "household" income only – which can include a stepparent and exclude a biological parent. Always read the find print and call the college for specific details.

To calculate costs, a **Net Price Calculator (NPC)** is a good place to start. All college websites have Net Price Calculators. Some colleges have their own and some use a licensed federal model. It is a good idea to have your recent taxes and financial statements at hand to answer questions and get more accurate data. (Federal NPC website: https://nces.ed.gov/ipeds/netpricecalculator/#/).

Considerations Regarding Early Decision Applications with Financial Aid
If you apply early decision to your favorite school, do not forget to complete the CSS Profile form by the same date as the application deadline. You will need the financial aid information in order to make an informed decision on whether you can commit. If you do not receive the amount of aid that you expected, you may either appeal to the financial aid office or you can withdraw your application. Note that lack of funding is the only way you can withdraw from an Early Decision commitment.

Other terms to be aware of when indicating to colleges that you are applying financial aid are:

- **Need-Blind**
  Where you see 'need-blind' indicated, it means that an admission decision is separate (blind) from the financial aid process. The admissions application is evaluated, a decision is made, and those accepted are then sent to the financial aid office for review.

- **Need-Aware**
  Where you see 'need-aware' indicated, an admission decision *can* be sensitive to the financial need of the applicant. Many schools admit that they are budget-conscious when accepting a freshman class and, as such, need-aware assessment can mean that financial aid applicants could be placed on a wait list rather than outright acceptance.

- **Gapping**
  This is a process of admitting a student while providing a financial package that does not fully meet the calculated need.

The Financial Aid Package

Financial Aid packages come in all shapes and forms. Many schools do not give you the bottom line of what you will pay when all costs are calculated. It is advisable to calculate the basic costs of the school and add up the various components of the aid package to see if it will work for you and your family.

Usual College Breakdown for Awards

- **Self-Help**
  This may include an opportunity to work on campus through a Federal work-study program, Federal (Stafford) loans, and/or school loans.

- **Grants**
  If the college meets 10% of your need, the remaining amount can be filled with grants, which do not need to be paid back. These are a combination of federal grants or grants from the actual funds of the college.

- **Merit Awards**
  These may also be a part of an award in the form of a scholarship that goes beyond the actual need of a student. It may even be awarded to a student not applying for financial aid in the hope of attracting top scholars to that school.

The bad news is time flies. The good news is you're the pilot.

– *Michael Altshuler*

4.5 PARENT POINTER – HELP WITH THE APPLICATIONS

You can help your teen with the application by:

- *Having personal, professional, academic, and financial information on hand for applications and financial aid documentation;*

- *In some applications, including the Common Application, there is an option for an applicant to submit an 'explanatory essay.' If your teen has had any disruption to their high school education or if they have had an illness or family circumstance that may have hindered their progress, they can be described in this essay. You can help your teen by discussing with them how to approach this essay.*

- *You can help in the essay-writing phase of the applications by brainstorming ideas and proof reading. For more information on the best ways to help, see the next chapter.*

There are only two lasting bequests we can hope to give our children. One of these is roots, the other, wings.

— Johann Wolfgang von Goethe

CHAPTER 5

COLLEGE APPLICATION WRITING: ESSAYS, PERSONAL STATEMENTS, AND SUPPLEMENTS

Today you are You, that is truer than true. There is no one alive who is Youer than You

– Dr. Seuss

5.1   COLLEGE APPLICATION ESSAYS

A college applications admissions essay is a piece of writing written by an applicant to college. The college essay, also sometimes referred to as the personal statement, is the foundational piece of writing in a college application. The Common Application and other multi-school applications systems (such as the Coalition Application and the Universal Application) require a main essay or, in the case of the University of California system for example, several essays. The terms college essay and personal statement are used interchangeably, but you should be aware that there is a difference between the styles of each. The college essay can be:

- **A narrative essay** is a story that describes an experience that reveals the student's personality and the development of personal understanding and growth through that experience.

- **A personal statement** is an autobiographical account of your interests and intentions.

In reality, the Common Application essay prompts are broad and flexible enough to enable you to write an essay that combines both styles to great success. It is important to note, however, that the generic term 'college application essay' may refer to the two styles or a combination of both, but the requirement for a 'personal statement' may not. Remember to read directions carefully and always respond specifically to the prompt. Other pieces of writing to be considered in college applications are:

Supplementary Writing and Essays are college-specific and in addition to the main application essay. Supplements often take the form of college or department specific prompts to give applicants the opportunity to demonstrate their knowledge and interest in a school or subject and a chance to promote their suitability and 'fit' for the college.

Scholarship essays are similar to personal statements in that they often require explanation of an applicant's circumstances, abilities, and personal qualities. The most common scholarship essay prompt is on the subject of leadership and an applicant should demonstrate their leadership abilities in the essay through description of activities and experiences.

Explanatory Essay(s) are optional. The Common Application has a section in which you can write about something you believe is relevant to your application that has not been possible to say anywhere else. In this essay, you can describe **challenges you have faced** or are facing, such as:

> Financial difficulties;
> Prejudice;
> Social disenfranchisement;
> Learning disabilities;
> Physical disabilities;
> Family problems;
> Medical problems;
> Unexpected tragedies.

The essays and supplements are your one DIRECT personal link to the admissions officers. Even your interview is indirect because it is transmitted to the admissions office via the interviewer's report. The essay and supplements are therefore, the only aspects of the application over which you have the most control. This is the opportunity to give the reader sense of who you are - your values, perspectives, and

COLLEGE APPLICATION WRITING: ESSAYS, PERSONAL STATEMENTS, AND SUPPLEMENTS

what makes you tick. The best essays are those that an admissions officer would describe as reflective, thoughtful, and well written.

As you think about all the writing you are about to do, it will be helpful to think about what it is you actually want college admissions officers to know about you. You will have completed your application with information on your academic qualifications and extracurricular activities, but do these express who you really are? Personal qualities and skills are the attributes that make you, YOU, and are important factors to college admissions officers who want to know more about you.

Be honest with yourself and think about your personal qualities and skills. Personal quality is a characteristic of your personality, such as kindness or optimism, and a skill is the ability to do something well, such a computer programming or singing. One way to think about your own qualities is to imagine what it is others say about you. How do you think a friend might describe you to his or her parents, for example? Your qualities may not be the things you think they are. Qualities can be simply things you do automatically and naturally because they define who you are. But, in a different context, and to others, your qualities are special and may be the very thing that separates you from other applicants. The table below indicates qualities and skills:

Personal Qualities	Personal Skills
Calm	Analyze information
Confident	Play a sport
Sensitive	Read a map
Punctual	Communication
Responsible	Design/creating
Conscientious	Recall facts
Strong minded	Public speaking
Team worker	Repair machines
Determined	First Aid
Hard working	Art
Trustworthy	Singing
Well organized	Solve problems
Enterprising	Research
Friendly	Speak languages (Bilingual)
Leadership ability	Photography
Enthusiastic	Computer skills
Adaptable	Manage money
Patient	Mental arithmetic
Imaginative	Play a musical instrument

If you are reading this book and preparing to apply to college, you know better than anyone that all of this didn't just 'happen:' You have worked very hard to get to this point in your life. Think of those endless hours of homework, studying for standardized tests, and playing on the JV basketball team. All of those things show that you have incredible qualities, such as, for example, tenacity, perseverance, endurance, and stamina. These are qualities that colleges want to know about. The student who can stick with their studies and see them through to the end is special. A well-written essay showing these aspects of your personality – if you have them – will give the admissions readers a good sense of who you are and of what you are capable. Other qualities that may not be immediately apparent include:

- Having a philosophical approach to life is an under-recognized and appreciated quality in a teenager. People who question the status quo, think outside of the box, or who are simply curious about the world, are interesting, engaged people in whom admissions officers will be interested;

- Strength and courage are admirable qualities in any individual. The teen who has gone against the crowd, who has fought for something better for themselves or for others, is someone who college admissions officers will notice;

- Compassion and commitment are also admirable qualities and yet, are difficult to write about convincingly without coming across as sanctimonious. If your volunteer activity is to do the grocery shopping every week for an elderly lady, this is the *activity*, but it is not the *experience*. Perhaps you spend an extra half an hour chatting and drinking tea with the lady *because you want to*, because the lady reminds you of your grandma who passed away last year, or because she is interesting and funny. Indicating the details of the experience and your personal feelings about it tell them much more about you than simply saying that you do the grocery shopping every week. Anyone can do that, but not everyone has the compassion, interest, and patience to spend that extra time to go beyond requirements or expectations. This is the *experience* that shows college admissions who you actually are, not what you do.

You may have had the opportunity to list your skills in your application, in which case it is redundant (and unwise) to do so again in your essay. However, you can include in your essay stories related to how you used your skill(s) in specific ways. Below is a table to help you think about your own qualities and skills and how you have demonstrated them:

Qualities	Skills
Quality 1: Evidence:	Skill 1: Evidence:
Quality 2: Evidence:	Skill 2: Evidence:

5.2 THE WRITING PROCESS – THE BASICS

Thinking about the process

1. Stay calm and focused: Remember, this is the part of the application over which you have total control;
2. Do not write your essay at the last minute. This is an important part of the application and you must leave yourself enough time to be able to think about it for a while, talk about it with others if you wish, and then actually write it, leave it for a while, and come back to it;

COLLEGE APPLICATION WRITING: ESSAYS, PERSONAL STATEMENTS, AND SUPPLEMENTS

3. Pay close attention to specific instructions, such as word count minimum and maximum, theme or focus of essay required, and, of course, the exact requirements of the questions or prompts;
4. If you have any questions (the answers to which you cannot find on the college website or from your counselor), do not be afraid to call the college admissions office. It is really important that you understand exactly what is required of you.

Focusing Your Thoughts and Choosing Your Topic

1. Think about what the college is actually asking. It is really important that your essay answers the question or prompt, but it must also tell your own story;
2. Just because the topic might be interesting does not mean that an essay on that topic can be interesting. The best way to do this is to relate a specific incident, event, or experience in which you played a part and/or on which you have an opinion. The essay should show how you engaged in the event;
3. Write about something that is important to YOU and you alone. Stay focused on your experience and your engagement and thoughts;
4. Don't try to second-guess the college admissions office by thinking about what they would like or what they want to hear. Instead, think about what you want to tell them and what you want them to know about you.

Starting to Write

1. Work in Word or Pages and cut and paste into the application when your essay is completely finished;
2. Do not try to cover too much. An essay that covers too much material will end up too long or, if shorter, superficial. Do not generalize, but think about being specific and detailed: your essay will be more entertaining - and successful;
3. Be personal. This is your opportunity to show who you are beyond your academic qualifications and to give the college admissions officers a glimpse into how you think. Remember that the admissions officers are trying to get to know you through your own words. Even if your subject is an academic one, you should show your personal engagement with the subject through personal experiences, observations, and opinions;
4. Express your feelings. If you are passionate about a subject, convey it. If you feel strongly about something, express your feelings on it. Expressing your feelings breathes life into your essay;
5. Don't try to be something you're not. Write on a subject that feels 'right' to you, and express your thoughts and feelings in a natural way. Try not to use vocabulary that you would not use in the real world (or in the real world of an essay). Always read your essay out aloud to yourself and listen for words or phrases that sound awkward, unnecessary, or pompous;
6. Be reflective and write in depth. When you write on one theme, subject, or experience, you are more able to be specific and detailed. When you have decided on your topic, think about responding to the questions:
   - WHY? - Why do I want to be an engineer?
   - HOW? - How did I reach the decision to study English literature?

   Concentrate on responding to these questions rather than, What?, When?, or Where? questions;
7. Write carefully. Think about structure of your essay and the flow of ideas, making each sentence a progression of the last. Pay attention to grammar and do not rely only on spell check;
8. Think about how to get in as much relevant information as you can. Use the following rubric as a guide:

CONTENT AND SCOPE OF THE ESSAY	
Category	**Ways to demonstrate in the essay**
Track Record	Clear statement of your interest and demonstration of experience or track record in that field. If you like debate, indicate that you have been on the school's debate team and even discuss topic(s)
Study Interest(s)	Clear statement of interest, i.e., if you discuss your passion for engineering, make sure that ALL the colleges to which you are applying have engineering programs
Contribution & Diversity	Clear statement of how you can enhance college diversity (academic, athletic, artistic, that school may not have (e.g. a girl contributing to engineering or physics, a boy pursuing nursing or dance)
Focus	Indication of the variety of interests that are meaningful to you, potentially with the idea to develop and build expertise in college
Prestige	Indicate if you bring prestige/celebrity to the school, e.g. you have published book, had a photography exhibition, or you are a known actor or athlete
Legacy	Indicate if you are a child of alumni (Legacy students earn points for this aspect in the 'why do you want to come here?' essay, but you can certainly mention it in your essay if relevant to your story)
Special Qualities & Leadership	Indicate if you do something out of the ordinary or 'special' that would fulfill a college's need, e.g. you play the harp or bassoon (for the orchestra), are a lacrosse champion (for an emerging lacrosse program), have studied Ancient Greek in high school (for academic excellence)
Character	Indicate that you possess character. If you have emerged from a difficult situation and demonstrated exceptional character (e.g. high principles, values, ethics, etc.)

Finishing your essay

1. Read your essay out aloud. Sometimes, reading backwards (as in sentence by sentence, not word by word!) can be a great way to catch grammatical errors. Accuracy in spelling and punctuation are vital. You don't want to upset your reader with mistakes that could have so easily been avoided;
2. Ask one or two trusted people to look over your essay, but do not allow them to revise or change it. They can make comments, but *you* must revise it yourself if you feel they make good points. This is YOUR essay and it is YOUR integrity at stake;
3. When it is finished, cut and paste it into your application, ensuring that the word count is correct and that it fits into the box perfectly.

5.3   THE COMMON APPLICATION ESSAY

There are seven essay prompts on the Common Application, from which a student chooses one and writes an essay of up to 650 words. The prompts are concisely worded and the subjects broad enough to enable the writer to find something to which they can respond. These are the prompts as they appear in the 2019-2020 Common Application:

COLLEGE APPLICATION WRITING: ESSAYS, PERSONAL STATEMENTS, AND SUPPLEMENTS

1. Some students have a background, identity, interest, or talent that is so meaningful they believe their application would be incomplete without it. If this sounds like you, then please share your story.
2. The lessons we take from obstacles we encounter can be fundamental to later success. Recount a time when you faced a challenge, setback, or failure. How did it affect you, and what did you learn from the experience?
3. Reflect on a time when you questioned or challenged a belief or idea. What prompted your thinking? What was the outcome?
4. Describe a problem you've solved or a problem you'd like to solve. It can be an intellectual challenge, a research query, an ethical dilemma - anything that is of personal importance, no matter the scale. Explain its significance to you and what steps you took or could be taken to identify a solution.
5. Discuss an accomplishment, event, or realization that sparked a period of personal growth and a new understanding of yourself or others.
6. Describe a topic, idea, or concept you find so engaging that it makes you lose all track of time. Why does it captivate you? What or who do you turn to when you want to learn more?
7. Share an essay on any topic of your choice. It can be one you've already written, one that responds to a different prompt, or one of your own design.

5.3.1 GUIDELINES ON THE COMMON APPLICATION ESSAY

Below are suggestions on how to approach each of the essay prompts:

COMMON APPLICATION ESSAY PROMPT # 1
Some students have a background or story that is so central to their identity that they believe their application would be incomplete without it. If this sounds like you, then please share your story.

This prompt gives you the opportunity to share a story that reveals how the story has made you the person you are today. Everyone has had events, people, or circumstances in their lives that have somehow shaped their individual personalities.

The first step is to think about what the prompt is really asking. It is actually so broad that, to a certain extent, it gives you permission to write about anything. You must be careful, though, not to make your response too broad. The story you tell needs to be one that you recognize and can articulate as being "central to [your] identity" and as being important enough that you application "would be incomplete without it."

Defining "central to your identity"
What is it that makes you, you? Is it your great sense of humor? Your competitive spirit? What do admire most about yourself? What makes you different from other people? Make a list of everything you know about yourself, taking into consideration the following:

- Think about how others might describe you. Look at yourself through their eyes and think about what it is they like about you. Your best friend might describe you as loyal. How does he or she know that? What happened to make him or her think you are loyal?

- When are you your 'best self?' Do you find yourself at your best when you are working at the coffee shop on a Saturday morning? Perhaps it's because you love being around people, you like the responsibility, or you like the smell of coffee. Somewhere in your reasoning may be the start of your story;

- Your 'background' may be the basis of your story. Did you grow up in an unusual place or in challenging circumstances? Did you live in a multi-ethnic community and exposed to different ideas, languages, faiths, and food? Did you or a family member have significant challenges to overcome? Do you have an obsession or passion that has influenced your life and decisions? When writing, remember to relate your story to YOU and your thoughts and feelings about the experience;

- Who are your role models? What do you admire about them? How have they influenced your behavior and aspirations? Remember, if you write about a role model to always reference how YOU were/are influenced by them. The story is about you, not them;

- Diversity is a valued aspect of college life. If you come from a diverse background, and have a story to tell about how it felt being 'different' and how it has influenced your life and your decisions, that is your story;

- Your story may be about your past, but you should reflect on it in relation to your present and how that story has made you the interesting and passionate individual who is ready to contribute to the college community;

- Do not waste this opportunity to say something interesting about yourself by repeating activities or stories that you have elsewhere in the application. After reading your essay, the college admissions officers should have a sense of who you are, what interests you, and how you will be an asset to the freshman class they are building;

- Remember, this essay is about you, but it is also about your writing style. When you have finished writing, make sure you read it out aloud to 'hear' awkward words and sentences, and then be meticulous about proof-reading several times.

COMMON APPLICATION ESSAY PROMPT #2
The lessons we take from obstacles we encounter can be fundamental to later success. Recount a time when you faced a challenge, setback, or failure. How did it affect you, and what did you learn from the experience?

This is a challenging prompt, giving you the opportunity to describe your ability to learn from failures and mistakes. Honesty and introspection are key to responding to this prompt and it is important to structure this essay in such a way that you allow plenty of space to give details and analysis on what you learned from the experience. If handled well, this essay can be successful and college admissions officers look favorably on an applicant who has taken the risk of revealing that they have failed in some way. In this essay, they want to see evidence that an applicant has:

- Grown and matured in the process of learning from the challenge, setback, or failure;
- Learned a valuable lesson that will potentially prepare them for future setbacks;
- Developed confidence and maturity that comes with triumphing over adversity.

COLLEGE APPLICATION WRITING: ESSAYS, PERSONAL STATEMENTS, AND SUPPLEMENTS

Defining Challenge, Setback, and Failure
A challenge and setback are similar in that they can both refer to obstacles out of your control, such as:

- A personal injury or sickness that stops you from competing in your favorite sport or keeping you away from school for weeks;
- Moving schools;
- A family member's illness and your help with care and support.

Failure refers to a personal action over which you have control, such as:

- Failure to apply yourself to your studies: Think about the factors that distracted and why they were so important to you at the time. Think about what happened to make you change your behavior;

- Failure to behave appropriately: Think about why you behaved the way you did and how you should have behaved. Think about the difference between your mindset then and now and the thought processes you went through to change your behavior;

- Failure to act: Think about why you did not act for something that was important to you. Was it fear of ridicule or embarrassment? Why did you lack the conviction to act? Consider also what you wish you had done;

- Failing a friend or family member: If you were unkind or disloyal, think about why you behaved that way at the time. Consider how you came to terms with your actions and what you have done to make amends;

- A lapse in judgment: If you did something foolish or dangerous, think about what you were trying to achieve and why. Think about how you came to understand that you need to act more responsibly.

Analyze the question
The lessons we take from obstacles we encounter can be fundamental to later success. Recount a time....
You need to describe the obstacle that you are going to analyze. Keep in mind that your goal is to demonstrate the lessons you learned from experiencing that obstacle that led you to success. Remember that success is not only about 'winning,' it's also about 'achieving' and your success may well be your achievement to have made it through high school with the grades and confidence to apply to college.

Decide on the obstacle itself. Did something happen to cause you to lose focus on school? Were you sick? Did you move and change schools? Whatever your obstacle, make a note of it at the top of the page and start to think of how you overcame that obstacle.

When you attempt to 'Recount a time' when you experienced the obstacle, Keep your language clear and concise (think of 'reporting' the obstacle without the emotional context that is required for analyzing it).

How did it affect you? It is really important that you think back to your initial reactions and try to evoke the exact emotions you experienced. Were you angry with yourself or others? Were you surprised, horrified, or ashamed by the failure? Be honest in describing exactly how you felt about the obstacle, even if you see in retrospect that you over-reacted or had trouble coming to terms with it.

What lessons did you learn? This is the crux of the essay and you should be prepared to analyze those initial feelings and put them into context with who you are today. You will need to ask yourself important questions, such as, 'Why did I behave so irrationally?' or 'What was it that made me turn the problem around?'

You now need to show your thoughtful introspection of the experience by describing your understanding of the lessons you learned, the insight you gained, and explanation of how they contributed to your personal growth. Remember, if your essay doesn't show that you have learned something valuable and that you are a better person because of your failure, the essay will not be successful.

COMMON APPLICATION ESSAY PROMPT #3
Reflect on a time when you challenged a belief or idea. What prompted you to act? Would you make the same decision again?

Successful essays using this prompt will be those that demonstrate conviction and passion for a belief or idea and honest reflection and critical thinking in discussing the question of whether or not you would make the same decision again.

Choosing an "Idea or Belief"
An idea or belief could be your own or it could be the idea or belief of a family, community, or country. Before you decide on an idea or belief, consider the purpose of this essay. The college admissions officers have access to your grades, test scores, and list of activities, and they have this essay as the only way to get a sense of who you really are. This essay prompt offers the opportunity for you to speak honestly about something you believe in; something that was important enough for you to act upon or against and in some way question the status quo. This essay requires careful handling and should show that you are a thoughtful, analytical, and committed person who cares deeply about something, but that 'something' must be carefully considered: writing about your beliefs on subjects with a strong political, ethical, or religious context, for example, could be controversial and potentially risky. A 'safer' way to approach this complex question is to discuss an action or experience that caused you to recognize the need for change and describe your actions and resulting outcome.

Analyze the Question
This prompt requires demonstration of intellectual curiosity and thoughtful debate. Read the question carefully and respond to each of the three distinct parts:

Reflect on a time when you challenged a belief or idea; To 'reflect' upon something you did is to *analyze* and *contextualize* your actions. What motivated you to act? Why did you feel change was necessary? What, exactly, did you do, to challenge the belief or idea? Was it an issue of its time or is it ongoing? How have your actions played a role in your personal growth?

What prompted you to act? What were your motives? Why did you do what you did? What were you thinking at the time? Was there a single event that caused you to take action? It is important that you reflect on *why* you acted rather merely describing *how* you acted.

Would you make the same decision again? Reflect on your feelings about the experience and whether or not you believe your actions to have been appropriate. What resulted from your challenge? In retrospect, was the outcome worth the effort? This is not an essay that calls for a satisfying conclusion, it is about

COLLEGE APPLICATION WRITING: ESSAYS, PERSONAL STATEMENTS, AND SUPPLEMENTS

articulating your thoughts and showing how you emerged from the experience with a greater understanding of yourself.

COMMON APPLICATION ESSAY PROMPT #4
Describe a problem you've solved or a problem you'd like to solve. It can be an intellectual challenge, a research query, an ethical dilemma - anything that is of personal importance, no matter the scale. Explain its significance to you and what steps you took or could be taken to identify a solution.

This prompt gives you that opportunity to write about a "problem" that is of "personal importance" to you, giving you scope to write on any issue that you believe needs to be solved. Whatever you write about, you must describe how your interest in the issue originated and evolved and why it is important to you.

Defining intellectual challenge, research query, or ethical dilemma
Although this prompt allows you to explore more academic and intellectual topics, it is important that you do not go into intensely intricate details of, say, Astrophysics or Mathematical formulae. Whilst it is admirable to demonstrate your passion and commitment, and perfectly acceptable to show that you know what you're talking about, you must be aware that the point of the essay, as with all the prompts, is to highlight *your* personality, identity, and how you think about the world.

Analyze the question
"No matter the scale"
This directive allows you to address ambitious, hypothetical problems that you believe need to be solved. You could address a global issue, such as global warming, for example, but you must be careful not to generalize: you must be specific and focus on one or two aspects that are important to you. Moreover, you must demonstrate and emphasize your own engagement with the problem.

You can also address a hypothetical (ethical) problem, such as, for example, the use of Artificial Intelligence in health care. If you choose to take this approach, make sure you frame the hypothetical problem clearly, explain why you consider it a problem, outline the important points, and explain your steps to create a solution.

Explain...the steps you took
Be sure to describe the event or experience that caused you to realize the extent and gravity of the problem, the specific actions you took to attempt to solve the problem, for example:

- Explanation on why solving your problem is so critical;
- Identification of the tangible change your solution would bring to people's lives;
- You specific actions, e.g., speaking at events, calling sponsors, raising money, designing advertising material.

COMMON APPLICATION ESSAY PROMPT #5
Discuss an accomplishment, event, or realization that sparked a period of personal growth and a new understanding of yourself or others.

In this self-analytical essay, you need to show your transition from one way of thinking to another and demonstrate through your essay that you are a strong, thoughtful college applicant.

Defining accomplishment, event, and realization
When thinking about an 'accomplishment or event,' the best choice will, of course, be a significant moment in your life. In this essay you can discuss something you value highly, which could be any number of things.

An accomplishment could be:
- You reached a goal that you set for yourself, e.g., a higher GPA, earned Eagle Scout or similar high-ranking distinction in an activity, published an essay or poem, etc;
- You did something independently for the first time, e.g., got a job, prepared a meal for the family, traveled by airplane on your own for the first time;
- You overcame a disability or handicap, e.g. a learning difference, a physical limitation, shyness, or anxiety;
- You worked alone or with a team to win an award, raise funds, or gain recognition in a particular field;
- You successfully launched your own business, e.g., a lawn mowing or babysitting business, a computer repair/rebuilding service, etc;
- You successfully removed yourself from a challenging situation, e.g., a toxic friend group, a situation in which your values were compromised;
- You did something physically challenging, e.g., ran a marathon, climbed a mountain, or changed your lifestyle habits to focus on your health;
- You were involved in a community or service project, e.g., instigating a pet visiting service to elderly care facilities or helping to build a house with Habitat for Humanity.

An Event could be:
- You passed a milestone in your life, such as your first day of high school or the first time you drove by yourself;
- You experienced a traumatic event, such as a personal accident or the loss of a loved one.

A realization could be:
- An interaction with someone (a friend, family member or stranger) that opens your eyes to an issue in a profound way;
- A world event, situation, or plight that inspired you to reflect upon your values and to think about your potential to help 'make a difference' in the world.

Analyze the question
Personal growth can stem from failure
The 'accomplishment, event, or realization' need not be a triumphant moment or, even a defining moment, in your life, but it does need to be something from which you learned something about yourself and/or others. An accomplishment could be triumphing over setbacks or failure, and an event could be losing a game or an embarrassing moment when you forgot your lines in the school play. The negative aspects of these types of accomplishments and events may lead you to evaluate if your story is more suitable for a response to Prompt #2. Either way, you will be demonstrating that failure – in whatever form – led you to you learn something about yourself, accept your shortcomings and overcome them, and ultimately to reflect on them to help you grow.

"Discuss"
When you "discuss" your event or accomplishment, do not spend too much time describing it, and ensure that you evaluate the outcome of it. This essay will be successful if you explore the *significance* of the accomplishment, event, or realization. You must analyze *how* the experience impacted you and *why* the experiences means so much to you.

COLLEGE APPLICATION WRITING: ESSAYS, PERSONAL STATEMENTS, AND SUPPLEMENTS

COMMON APPLICATION ESSAY PROMPT #6
Describe a topic, idea, or concept you find so engaging that it makes you lose all track of time. Why does it captivate you? What or who do you turn to when you want to learn more?

In some respects, this essay prompt is the most 'personal' of the prompts in that it uses words such as 'engaging' and 'captivate', which suggests that it invites you to analyze this topic, idea, or concept in relation not only to your feelings about it, but also in relation to how happy and content you are when engaging in it. The point of the essay, however, remains the same as all the essay prompts in that you need to show engagement with a subject in the form of WHY you are interested in it, WHAT you do to further that interest, and HOW it has contributed to making you the person you are.

If this prompt appeals to you, you probably already know exactly the topic, idea, or concept that is, "so engaging that it makes you lose all track of time." However, you should ask yourself the following questions to help you stay focused on what the question is actually asking and outline the best framework to suit your theme:

- What are the good – and bad – things that have come out of your engagement with this topic, idea, or concept?
- What did you learn about yourself along the way?
- Why does this topic, idea, or concept matter to you? To your family and/or community? To the world?
- Did learning about this topic, concept, or idea lead to other subjects that you find equally engaging?
- While learning more about your topic, concept, or idea, what did you learn about how you think and learn?
- Does this topic, concept, or idea, give you insight into what you most value in your life?
- Are you still engaged in learning about this topic, concept, or idea? If so, why is that a good thing? Are there any negative aspects to continuing with it?

This prompt provides a great opportunity to display writing prowess through specific descriptions, evocative words, and elegant style. The key to writing this essay is responding to the notion of why you are captivated by something. Remember, the most important aspect of this essay is that you REFLECT on the *experience* of your topic, idea, or concept, and DESCRIBE what you learned (and continue to learn) about yourself through your engagement with it.

COMMON APPLICATION ESSAY PROMPT #7
Share an essay on any topic of your choice. It can be one you've already written, one that responds to a different prompt, or one of your own design.

This is an open-ended prompt that allows you to express something that does not align directly with any of the other prompts. Writing your own question allows you to demonstrate individuality and confidence through engagement with a complex topic. This prompt allows you to be unconventional and, if done well, alerts the admissions officers that you may be different, interesting, and special. It allows for the more 'risky' essay, such as these successful examples:

- High-level discussion of a subject on which the applicant was particularly knowledgeable;
- Unusual stylistic creative devices, such as a philosophical metaphor to describe an applicant's four years of high school, or a poetic style to display an applicant's love for poetry;
- Humor, such as in an applicant's essay about overcoming a mortal fear of snakes.

Remember, whatever you choose to write in response to this prompt, the essay should demonstrate something meaningful about you, whether it is your personality, thought process, or values.

5.4 MAIN ESSAYS ON OTHER APPLICATIONS

The other multi-college applications systems also have a main essay or essays for an applicant to write, all of which follow along similar lines as the main Common Application essay.

5.4.1 THE COALITION APPLICATION ESSAY

The Coalition Application offers five essay prompts from which an applicant chooses one. They are along similar lines as the Common Application essay prompts and you can therefore use the notes related to those to help you think about how to respond to these prompts. There is no official maximum word count, but 500-550 words are recommended. The Coalition Application essay prompts are:

1. **Tell a story from your life, describing an experience that either demonstrates our character or helped to shape it.**
Use notes on Common App essay prompt #1 for guidance on how to approach this essay.
2. **Describe a time when you made a meaningful contribution to others in which the greater good was your focus. Discuss the challenges and rewards of making your contribution.**
Use notes on Common App essay prompts #3 and #4 for guidance on how to approach this essay.
3. **Has there been a time when you've had a long-cherished or accepted belief challenged? How did you respond? How did the challenge affect your beliefs?**
Use notes for Common App essay prompt #3 for guidance on how to approach this essay.
4. **What's the hardest part of being a teenager now? What's the best part? What advice would you give a younger sibling or friends (assuming they would listen to you)?**
Use notes for Common App essay prompts #2, #4, and #5 for guidance on how to approach this essay.
5. **Submit an essay on a topic of your choice.**
Use notes for Common App essay prompt #7 for guidance on how to approach this essay.

5.4.2 THE UNIVERSAL APPLICATION PERSONAL STATEMENT

The Universal Application requires a Personal Statement of 650 words maximum and an Activity Description of 100-150 words. You can use notes from Common App essay prompts to help you think about responding to these too. As with the Common and Coalition Applications, many of the member colleges also require their own college-specific essays.

> **The Personal Statement** - Please write an essay that demonstrates your ability to develop and communicate your thoughts. Some ideas include: a person you admire; a life-changing experience; or your viewpoint on a particular current event.
> Use notes from Common App essay prompts #1, #2, and #4 for guidance on how to approach this essay.
>
> **Activity Description** - Tell us about one of your extracurricular, volunteer, or employment activities.
> Use notes from Common App essay prompts #1 and #6 for guidance on how to approach this essay.

COLLEGE APPLICATION WRITING: ESSAYS, PERSONAL STATEMENTS, AND SUPPLEMENTS

5.4.3 UNIVERSITY OF CALIFORNIA APPLICATION PERSONAL INSIGHT ESSAYS

There are eight Personal Insight questions from which the applicant must choose four, all of a maximum of 350 words in length. The University of California application site indicates that all questions are equal and are given equal consideration in the application review process, which means that there is no advantage or disadvantage to choosing certain questions over others. It also indicates that there is no right or wrong way to answer the questions and that the focus is on getting to know the applicant's personality, background, interests, and achievements in your own unique voice. Helpfully, the application also provides writing guidelines and considerations for each prompt, which are outlined below:

1. Describe an example of your leadership experience in which you have positively influenced others, helped resolve disputes, or contributed to group efforts over time.
A leadership role can mean more than just a title. It can mean being a mentor to others, acting as the person in charge of a specific task, or taking lead role in organizing an event or project. Think about your accomplishments and what you learned from the experience.

- What were your responsibilities?
- Did you lead a team?
- How did your experience change your perspective on leading others?
- Did you help to resolve an important dispute at your school, church in your community or an organization?

Your leadership role doesn't necessarily have to be limited to school activities. For example, do you help out or take care of your family?

2. Every person has a creative side, and it can be expressed in many ways: problem solving, original and innovative thinking, and artistically, to name a few. Describe how you express your creative side.

- What does creativity mean to you?
- Do you have a creative skill that is important to you?
- What have you been able to do with that skill?
- If you used creativity to solve a problem, what was your solution?
- What are the steps you took to solve the problem?
- How does your creativity influence your decisions inside or outside the classroom?
- Does your creativity relate to your major or a future career?

3. What would you say is your greatest talent or skill? How have you developed and demonstrated that talent over time?
If there's a talent or skill that you're proud of, this is the time to share it. You don't necessarily have to be recognized or have received awards for your talent (although if you did and you want to talk about, feel free to do so).

- Why is this talent or skill meaningful to you?
- Does the talent come naturally or have you worked hard to develop this skill or talent? -Does your talent or skill allow you opportunities in or outside the classroom?
- If so, what are they and how do they fit into your schedule?

4. Describe how you have taken advantage of a significant educational opportunity or worked to overcome an educational barrier you have faced.
An educational opportunity can be anything that has added value to your educational experience and better prepared you for college. For example, participation in an honors or academic enrichment program, or enrollment in an academy that's geared toward an occupation or a major, or taking advanced courses that interest you — just to name a few.

- If you choose to write about educational barriers you've faced, how did you overcome or strive to overcome them?
- What personal characteristics or skills did you call on to overcome this challenge?
- How did overcoming this barrier help shape who are you today?

5. Describe the most significant challenge you have faced and the steps you have taken to overcome this challenge. How has this challenge affected your academic achievement?
A challenge could be personal, or something you have faced in your community or school. This is a good opportunity to talk about any obstacles you've faced and what you've learned from the experience.

- Why was the challenge significant to you?
- Did you have support from someone else or did you handle it alone?

If you're currently working your way through a challenge, what are you doing now, and does that affect different aspects of your life? For example, ask yourself, "How has my life changed at home, at my school, with my friends, or with my family?"

6. Think about an academic subject that inspires you. Describe how you have furthered this interest inside and/or outside of the classroom.
Discuss how your interest in the subject developed and describe any experience you have had inside and outside the classroom — such as volunteer work, summer programs, participation in student organizations and/or activities — and what you have gained from your involvement.

- Has your interest in the subject influenced you in choosing a major and/or career?
- Have you been able to pursue coursework at a higher level in this subject (honors, AP, International Baccalaureate (IB), college, or work)?

7. What have you done to make your school or your community a better place?
Things to consider: Think of community as a term that can encompass a group, team or a place – like your high school, hometown, or home. You can define community as you see fit, just make sure you talk about your role in that community.

- Was there a problem that you wanted to fix in your community?
- Why were you inspired to act?
- What did you learn from your effort?
- How did your actions benefit others, the wider community or both?
- Did you work alone or with others to initiate change in your community?

8. Beyond what has already been shared in your application, what do you believe makes you stand out as a strong candidate for admissions to the University of California?
Don't be afraid to brag a little. Even if you don't think you're unique, you are. Remember, there's only one of you in the world.

- From your point of view, what do you feel makes you belong on one of UC's campuses?
- When looking at your life, what does a stranger need to understand in order to know you?
- What have you not shared with us that will highlight a skill, talent, challenge, or opportunity that you think will help us know you better? We're not necessarily looking for what makes you unique compared to others, but what makes you, YOU.

5.5 CHOOSING A STYLE FOR YOUR ESSAY

5.5.1 The Narrative Essay

A narrative essay is a piece of writing which tells a story. In the case of a college application essay, the story should be about you. The primary purpose of a narrative essay is to share an experience that allows the college admissions officer to relate to you in some way, and thereby get a sense of who you are. There can be other characters in the story, but they are only written about in relation to your experience and to your understanding of your response (feelings) to that experience. A good narrative essay has the following components:

Chronology
A narrative essay of the required word length for college applications works well when written in a clear, preferably chronological, order. The story should develop smoothly from description of experience to revelation of responses and feelings about the experience, to a final exposition of what the experience means to you.

Stylistic Devices
A narrative essay allows you to use descriptive language that gives the story depth and makes it exciting to read.

Moral of the Story
The primary goal of a narrative essay is a moral to the story: It must have a satisfying conclusion showing what you learned from the experience (the story) and how it influenced you. The reader must come away from the essay with the satisfaction of knowing how you benefitted from the experience. When you write a narrative essay:

- You should try to involve the readers in your story. Being specific about events or deeds will allow them to engage more fully in your experience. For example, instead of, "I cleaned my dad's barbeque" you could say, "As a special treat for Father's Day, I surprised my dad by scrubbing every inch of his barbeque until it shone like new." Specific details such as 'Father's Day,' and your 'scrubbing' the barbeque 'until it shone like new' provide context and imagery. From these a reader can get a sense of you and might surmise you are probably a thoughtful person who takes time to do a job well;

- Don't be afraid to use 'I' – this is a story about you – but try to avoid starting every sentence with it. You can say things such as, "Being a keen tennis player, I.....", or "Knowing that the competition was ahead, I.....", or "Having earned enough money to travel, I....;"

- You should use generalizations at the end of your story. This helps your reader understand your point of view and see you as a person who understands the wider repercussions of experiences. A conclusion to the essay about cleaning the barbeque, for example, could be: 'To see how thrilled my Dad was with his 'present' made me realize that money cannot buy happiness and that, sometimes, even the smallest gestures can be the most valued.'

COLLEGE APPLICATION WRITING: ESSAYS, PERSONAL STATEMENTS, AND SUPPLEMENTS

Structure of a Narrative Essay

To get started, it is useful to outline your essay using a simple 5- paragraph structure to help you organize your thoughts and ensure that there is a progression of ideas throughout, as follows:

	Structure of a Narrative Essay
Paragraph 1	Introduction: An interesting 'hook' (opening line) to catch the reader's attention and introduce the topic/incident you are going to describe. Define your thesis and why it is important to you. Finish the paragraph by briefly describing what you learned as a result of the incident.
Paragraph 2	Broad description of event - where it happened, why it happened. Include details of other people involved.
Paragraph 3	Specific description of MY involvement in incident - why was I involved? What was I doing?
Paragraph 4	My reaction to the incident. Why it matters? What did I learn?
Paragraph 5	Conclusion: Refer to opening. How did your experience influence/impact your understanding of the incident and the 'bigger picture'?

Reasons why a narrative essay can be unsuccessful:

- There is no relationship between the story and lesson learned;
- It is too general;
- It lacks focus;
- It fails to show the writer's personality, thoughts, and/or feelings;
- The 'incident' lacks detail and specificity.

5.5.2   THE PERSONAL STATEMENT

A personal statement is your opportunity to explain to colleges why you have applied for the course(s) that you want to study. You need to demonstrate your enthusiasm and commitment, and convince the admissions officers that you would be an asset to their college. Remember, because you are indicating a specific area of academic interest, the admissions officers reading your statement will want to know why you chose the subject and wish to study it at a higher level. The simplest way to start is to break the statement down into 3 basic steps:

- Why you chose the college, program, and/or major;
- How you have furthered your interest through study, projects, research, internships, etc;
- Summarize how your interest, knowledge, and experiences led to choosing this course.

Although this is not a set structure for a personal statement, it may be a useful starting point when you begin drafting. You should refer to the program in which you are interested and indicate your excitement for further study at the college level. This will give the college admissions officers a sense of your potential to contribute to their academic community. In a personal statement, the admissions officers are looking for evidence that:

- You have chosen the right subject for the right reasons;
- You are mature enough to live and study at college;
- You have a range of interests and abilities;
- You have articulated well your depth of interest in the subject;
- You have studied independently.

Keep in mind that, although the majority of your essay should cover WHY you have chosen the course, there are certain points that you should include, such as:

- Reasons why that subject area interests you;
- Aspects of your current studies relating to the subject that reveal a strong 'narrative' or 'story' about your interests and abilities;
- Details of jobs, placements, work experience or voluntary work that you have undertaken, particularly if it has relevance to your chosen field;
- Hobbies, interests, and social activities that demonstrate you are a well-rounded person;
- Non-accredited qualifications, e.g. Scouting honors (Eagle Scout), public art display, article in a local newspaper, piano grade reached, student council representative, and any other achievements of which you are proud;
- Attributes that make you interesting, special, or unique;
- Whether you have any future plans of how you want to use your degree, and the knowledge and experience that you will gain;
- Why you think you would be a good student.

COLLEGE APPLICATION WRITING: ESSAYS, PERSONAL STATEMENTS, AND SUPPLEMENTS

There is no required structure for a personal statement, but certainly a good starting point is to outline a structure of 5 paragraphs of equal length, made up as follows:

	Structure of a Personal Statement
Paragraph 1	Subject introduction and controlling theme: My interests in the subject and how I reached the decision to study it at college
Paragraph 2	Related activities that you have done and your career aspirations
Paragraph 3	Descriptions of the skills and qualities you possess in relation to your chosen area of study, with examples
Paragraph 4	Other information related to extracurricular activities, interests, and hobbies, etc., preferably relating your skills to the subject
Paragraph 5	Conclusion: expand your overall theme without summarizing or repeating what you have already written and give reasons why you are a suitable candidate for the academic program

Reasons why a personal statement can be unsuccessful:

- It does not strongly support your stated 'area of interest' or major;
- It does not show sufficient understanding, relevance, or knowledge about the subject area;
- It lacks evidence of accurate understanding of or motivation for subject;
- It does not express a strong enough interest in the subject area.

5.6 THE DOS AND DON'TS OF COLLEGE ESSAY WRITING

DO	DO NOT
Be Specific	Write about adversities that aren't adverse
Write out abbreviations first time	Substitute an essay for a poem, art, or photo
Write about academic relevance	Bad-mouth anyone or anything
Explain terms/words where necessary	Show prejudice or bias
Use humor carefully	Send a previously written essay
Say only good things about yourself	Reveal family secrets (or any secrets)
Show your leadership	Write that you are like everyone else
Keep it to a good length	Write about foolish risks
Quantify achievements	Friends (what they did and think)
Tell a story showing 'you'	Send gimmicks
Indicate the prompt you are answering	Write about losing
Echo your values	Write about luxury vacations
Use your own vocabulary	Copy anyone else's work
Use your own 'voice'	Write about old news (4 years max)
	Write about politics (unless specific interest)
	Write about your pranks or tricks
	Write about religion (unless your subject)
	Write about drugs
	Write travel essays
	Write a piece with unresolved ending
	Whine or complain

The college application essay requires a style of writing with which most high school students are unfamiliar. Students can be caught off guard by the seemingly simplistic and prompts and the 'invitation' for honest expression. The most common problems that students encounter when getting started and after writing their first draft tend to be:

- Not knowing what to write about;
- Belief that they don't have a 'story' worthy of a college application essay;
- Understanding the necessity for relevance;
- Not being used to writing about themselves or their accomplishments;
- Difficulty in structuring their essay;
- Putting in too much information and too many irrelevant details;
- Repetition;
- Not responding to the prompt;
- Using language they think makes them sound clever;
- Responding in a way that they think a college wants to hear;
- Not being authentic;
- Not focusing on their strengths;
- Mistaking 'personal' to mean 'confessional' and writing about something that is too intimate (such as their struggles with an eating disorder, or their constant fighting with a parent);
- Believing that the word count is the target, rather than the maximum.

COLLEGE APPLICATION WRITING: ESSAYS, PERSONAL STATEMENTS, AND SUPPLEMENTS

It is important that you think about what is expected of you. Essentially, every successful college essay:

- Is thoughtful and honest: A strong essay is reflective and demonstrates that you have thought about and gained a clear perspective on your experiences and what you want in your future. It SHOWS the college admissions officer reader what they should know about you. Remember that the focus of the essay is YOU, your achievements, your obstacles, your goals, and your values;

- Is specific and focused: A good essay is not a list of your accomplishments. It is about putting your accomplishments and achievements IN CONTEXT with your life and experience. The college admissions officer is interested in how your experience demonstrates the theme of your essay;

- Is well structured and well written: College admissions officers expect an applicant's essay to be of the highest quality with no spelling or grammar errors. A bonus is when a student uses precise and vivid language and has well-organized and cohesive structure;

- Answers the question and/or responds to the prompt: It is so important to examine the essay prompt or question and to write an essay that explicitly responds to it. If the prompt asks you to describe a challenge you faced, you must use language that enables the reader to visualize your story to get a sense of who you are, how you overcame the challenge, and why the story is important to you;

- Shows development and 'maturity': An excellent essay takes time and needs to develop. After writing your first draft, step away from it for a while. When you go back to it, read it out aloud and pay careful attention to parts of the essay that would benefit from better structure or explanation. You will also hear what 'works' and what does not;

- Contains a 'hook': College admissions officers read hundreds, maybe even thousands, of applications every application cycle, which means that an essay with a 'hook' – a catchy introduction - is one that gets noticed. If the rest of the essay develops from the hook in a strong and cohesive structure the language is precise and vivid, it is very likely to be an essay that stands out from those that start out with a more conventional opening sentence;

- Shows progression and growth: If you choose to write an essay about overcoming obstacles and challenges, then it is important that you show HOW you dealt with them, overcame them, and transformed them into positive influences in your life. For example, if your essay theme is "overcoming obstacles" and you earned a poor grade in a class, but went to a community college at night to repeat the course to earn a better grade, that shows perseverance, resilience, and determination; all qualities that a college admissions reader will see as positive attributes. In an essay that discusses obstacles and challenges, it is vital that you show them how you overcame them and what you have learned from the experience;

- Demonstrates your interest and knowledge in a subject: For students who are passionate about a particular subject to the extent that it has influenced their life choices, an essay that shows that passion and commitment can be very powerful;

- Exudes self-confidence: Colleges look for the best students who demonstrate their abilities to pursue their goals and be successful regardless of the college they attend. Self-confidence reveals itself through your description of lifelong interests, sustained commitment, and/or perseverance in the face of adversity.

5.7 COLLEGE-SPECIFIC SUPPLEMENTS

Many schools require supplementary pieces of writing, which can range from essays of 50 words to 500 words, single word answers, or #hashtags to describe yourself. The most common supplementary essays focus on WHY you want to go to that particular college, and WHAT you will contribute.

Supplemental essays are as important as the long essays. Not only are they a test of your ability to express yourself well in a succinct way, they are also used to determine how well you know the college and how suitable you are as an applicant. The best supplementary essays demonstrate that:

- You have researched the college and, where relevant, the areas of study in which you are interested;
- Given consideration to how your skills, abilities, and experience connects to the college and program.

Think of supplements like this: if an admissions reader has got to this stage in your application, you have not been put in the 'rejection' pile. Your application has impressed the admissions officers in some way. If you and other students all have the same grades and student profile, the writing components (along with the main essay of the application) take on enormous importance as the main differentiator between one student and another. So, it is important to consider WHAT the college WANTS from this piece of writing, and HOW this piece of writing will DIFFERENTIATE you from other applicants.

What Does the College WANT from this Piece of Writing?
A college really wants to know about YOU and what it is about their institution that: a) interests you, and b) will enable you to make a meaningful contribution to its community. The best way to write about what interests you is to find out EXACTLY what the school offers that does interest you. Remember that college is an institution of LEARNING above all else. Whilst it is wonderful that the college has beautiful grounds, a fantastic football team, and cool dorms, these are not the things to mention in anything longer than a sentence (if at all!). Yes, you can talk about the 'feeling' or atmosphere of the place, but try to keep in mind that the admissions people already know that their institution is awesome and they really want to know about YOU.

Research The School and/or Program
The first place to start is the college's website and Mission Statement. What about the college's ethos appeals to you? Think about the things you value most in life and how this particular college's ethos responds to those values. For example, Loyola Marymount University (LMU) California explains its ethos and desired outcome in one sentence:

Loyola Marymount University offers rigorous undergraduate, graduate, and professional programs to academically ambitious students committed to lives of meaning and purpose.

From this one sentence, there are key terms that would stand out to the student interested in this kind of school – rigorous...programs, academically ambitious students, and lives of meaning and purpose. You would not just reiterate these words in your supplementary essay, but you would indicate how one or all of these goals are relevant to you, and why.

COLLEGE APPLICATION WRITING: ESSAYS, PERSONAL STATEMENTS, AND SUPPLEMENTS

Another approach is to explore aspects of a school's academic offerings that 'speak' to you. If you are keen on engineering, neuroscience, or medieval history, go to the relevant department site and take a look through the home page first. On the home page, there will be links to a variety of information and articles on current research, student activities, speakers, workshops, and letters or blogs from students studying overseas. Read through them and choose two or three subjects, activities, or projects that appeal to you. Take note of the key elements of the articles, with information such as, names (with titles), dates, activities, locations, statements, type of work, publications, etc.

As an example, let's look at the Undergraduate Program of Neuroscience at Boston University (http://www.bu.edu/neuro/undergraduate/):

> *This program combines breadth of exposure to the field as a whole with the opportunity for depth of experience in one of three central domains of neuroscience: Cellular and Systems, Cognition and Behavior, and Computational Neuroscience.*

Consider the scope of the neuroscience program and the most appealing aspects to you by looking for clues in the department's description:

> *Neuroscience students will have access to the extensive resources and expertise of affiliated faculty across multiple departments and colleges throughout the university. A wide array of courses are offered through the departments of Biology, Chemistry, Computer Science, Mathematics & Statistics, Physics, Psychology, and Health Sciences in Sargent College. Together more than 50 upper level neuroscience electives are offered, including laboratory courses and seminars.*

The paragraph following describes further dimensions to the Neuroscience major:

> *Opportunities for independent laboratory research are available through multiple departments in the Colleges of Arts and Sciences and Engineering, and at Boston University School of Medicine, including Anatomy and Neurobiology, Biochemistry, Neurology, Pathology, Pharmacology & Experimental Therapeutics, Physiology and Biophysics, and Psychiatry. Undergraduate research opportunities in neuroscience laboratories expand throughout the university across both the Charles River and Medical campuses.*

The opportunities are vast and you can describe your interest in any one of these areas, focusing on WHAT and WHY you are interested in a particular area and HOW you see yourself pursuing it in college and contributing to the BU academic community.

Finally, look at the bottom of the page for student activities in the field. For example, one article on BU's Mind and Brain Society's third annual 'Bringing Recognition And Interest to Neuroscience Day' (B.R.A.I.N. Day) detailed how 60 undergraduate volunteers spent the day leading interactive activities for K-12 students, parents, teachers, and members of the BU community. If you like the sound of this kind of activity, you could indicate your interesting in participating in a society such as this, and even suggest ideas on how you could contribute.

Consider the 'Angle' You Want to Take

The Professor Angle - Another interesting area in department sites is the faculty. It is a good idea to research the professors in the field of interest, focusing on their current project and publications. If a particular professor's work is of interest, you could use that as the focus of your supplemental essay. Remember to say WHAT (the field is), WHO (is conducting it), WHY (it is important to you), and HOW (you would like to contribute).

The Contribution Angle - If you have had some experience in your field of interest (such as an internship or volunteer opportunity) and think that you want a career in this field, let the admissions reader know that. Specifically, let them know how you feel you could make a contribution to the field and ultimately, to the world at large.

The Exploratory Angle - If you are making more of a 'statement of interest' rather than a declaration of a major in a field of study, i.e. you don't want to make a 'commitment' to a major, explain WHY the subject is something you want to learn more about, HOW you became interested in this subject, and WHAT you think you might be able to contribute.

How Will This Piece of Writing Differentiate You from Other Students?

If you have followed through with the previous exercise, you will see that being SPECIFIC is key to a successful essay and it is this that will differentiate you from other students. By responding to the prompts in a specific and personal way, you are showing your personality, your academic curiosity, your integrity, and your enthusiasm - EVERYTHING that a college is looking for in a student. Moreover, you are showing your personal engagement with the college and giving a very clear sign that you want to attend.

Supplements Looking for 'Something Else'

Prompts that look for 'something else' tend to focus more on the personality and creative thinking of the applicant. Use them to your advantage to show admissions officers who you are, how you think, and what you can do. Just remember to be:

- Focused. Make sure you answer the question;
- Specific. Don't generalize. Don't ramble or repeat yourself. Every word counts;
- Authentic. Don't be afraid to show passion, enthusiasm and excitement for the program and/or college. Likewise, don't be afraid to show who you are, how you deal with issues, and what matters to you;
- True to yourself. Be who you are and show your strengths and how you will use them to be a productive member of the college community.

Supplements Looking for 'Good Fit' Applicants

Some supplementary essay prompts focus on why you and the college are a good match. Read the specific words on these prompts and think about what they want, which most often focuses on how you will fit into their campus. The best way to do this is to be specific and explain your engagement with the campus so far. For example, give specific examples from your visits, college fair talks with admissions officers, or emails with professors or current students..

Other Supplements

Words to Describe Yourself

Don't agonize over these. Think of your self-evaluation exercise and remember your strengths. Think about what you want most for admissions officers to know about you. Some good words to think about, depending on your personality, are: Energetic, Powerful, Focused, Target-Driven, Productive, Creative, Responsible, Well-organized, Thoughtful, Detailed, Patient, Diplomatic, Inclusive, Calm, Kind; Curious, Energetic, Optimistic, Innovative, Explorative. Whatever words you decide upon, think about what the admissions officer is thinking about you. Make every word say something positive about you.

Likes and Dislikes, and #Hashtags
There are no 'correct' answers to these prompts and you can be creative and thoughtful with them. Always think, though, about the image you are projecting: #justcruisinforfun is probably not a good idea, and #Cutesybunnylovesyou is not appropriate. Stanford University and the University of Southern California are amongst the colleges that have these prompts within their supplementary writing sections.

Activities and Experiences
Some colleges are now offering the option for applicants to submit an Activity Statement. Generally, in these statements, admissions officers are looking for evidence of prolonged engagement with an activity, with indications of initiatives and leadership.

Supplementary prompts often show you what type of college you are applying to and give you a clear picture of the college's expectations, helping you decide if it is actually the right choice for you. For example, Columbia is an extremely competitive Ivy League college. Columbia's supplementary prompts indicate Columbia's 'assumption' and 'expectations' of its applicants: LIST the books you are reading, What EXHIBITIONS have you visited over the past year, What PLAYS, THEATRE PRODUCTIONS have you seen in the past year? Columbia expects its students to be engaged in the world, intellectually curious, and mature.

Tips for Writing Supplements

- You are advised to take supplements VERY seriously. Most selective colleges on the Common Application have Writing Supplements and you should view them as great opportunities to promote yourself. Excellent essays can tip the scales when similarly qualified students are being assessed alongside each other;

- Evaluate your application as a whole and consider if the combined pieces are telling a story about you. Take a look at each written piece the college will receive from and about you—including your Common Application essay, your résumé, and your activities list – and see how they all come together as representative of you. Make sure you don't repeat yourself and write about something you have written about in the Common Application essay;

- Each Writing Supplement is unique. While all colleges will see your Common Application, only the individual colleges will see your Writing Supplement. Depending on the number of colleges to which you are applying, you may need to write a variety of supplemental essays. Each response is a new chance to tell a story about yourself and give a solid message of how you will engage in the academic community and what you can contribute to it;

- Be aware that some questions appear based on the answers you give about particular majors or merit scholarships. If you change your major or select 'no' to a particular program or scholarship, the prompt may disappear. Keep a running track of what you have to write for each supplement based on your Member Question selections (the essay tracker will help with this);

- Thoroughly research the colleges to which you apply. When making notes about each college (in the research phase of your college applications journey), think about what each college values. You can pick up important points by taking note of words that you see repeated through a college's marketing material and its mission statement. Always be thinking about how you can contribute to the college academic and campus community;

- Cut and paste from one essay to another wisely. Each supplement is separate and belongs to the individual college and you. The colleges do not communicate with each other, so you can reuse some of your essays, especially the longer ones and the optional activity statements. However, be very careful and make sure that you do not put an essay you have written for one college into the application for another college;

- Nothing is optional. Some colleges give you some optional essays and you should take advantage of them to offer new information. Every essay is a chance to demonstrate why you belong on that campus;

- Read each college's specific essay tips. Most colleges communicate their views on college essays and some even provide model essays. This is invaluable information to help you write a great essay that engages the admissions officers;

- The Common Application website offers college specific tips on the Member Questions and Writing Supplements and gives information about particular programs and links to more information within the Common Application website or to college websites;

- You can submit essays in two ways. Most colleges use the cut and paste method, but some require uploading of the essay as a document. All use word limits but some do not always tell you the word limit even after you paste in, so make sure that you use the Review function when you application is complete to ensure that that your entire essay is included.

5.8 WRITING FOR SCHOLARSHIPS, HONORS, AND SPECIAL PROGRAMS

Many private colleges offer scholarships for different reasons, but academic merit and financial need are the most common. Generally, colleges offer scholarship opportunities in three ways:

- Automatically considered for scholarship with application;
- Additional essay required for scholarship application;
- Invited at a later date to apply for scholarship (if criteria is met).

A creative and persuasive essay for scholarships, Honors College, or other special programs can make a student stand out from the crowd and give them the chance to be awarded monetary, academic, and extracurricular advantages. A formula for this type of targeted essay follows:

PREPARE
1 Answer the Question
Be sure that you are clear on <u>exactly</u> what the essay question is asking. If the prompt is interested in leadership, for example, dissect the question and ask yourself what the college actually wants:

- Is it asking for your definition of leadership?
- Is it asking how you how you exemplify leadership?
- Is it asking about leadership styles you admire?
- Is it asking about specific leaders you admire?
- Is it asking about how you will develop as a leader at their college?

The question may ask one or a combination of these questions. Whatever they ask, make sure that you ANSWER THE QUESTION!

2   Identify your audience
It is important that you identify your audience and that you relate it to the field of study to which you are applying. For example, if you are interested in Science, you could discuss a project or research that interests you, perhaps also in the context of work of the particular college. Keep in mind that the scholarship committee is looking for evidence of your engagement and your potential for contribution.

3   Consider the themes of the essay prompt
Underline the key theme(s) of the prompt. If the prompt uses terminology, such as diversity and/or innovation, make sure you incorporate those terms and evidence of your understanding of them in your essay. If you can, also indicate ways in which you have personally engaged in activities that enhanced your understanding of related ideas and concepts.

4   Research
Now you understand the requirements, research the subject, main themes, and concepts. If you can eloquently demonstrate your understanding, your essay will be successful.

WRITE
1   Define terms
It is helpful for the scholarship committee to see that you understand not only that there is a theme to the prompt, but also that you understand the theme. A brief description of your understanding of the main theme or a particular term will be appreciated.

2   Write a strong introduction
As with every other piece of writing you do, try to write an interesting opening to your essay. An engineering applicant might start an essay with: "As the robot's hand fell off, I knew it was back to the drawing board with the hardware genetic algorithm and that we were in for a long night of crisis management."

In this opening sentence, the robot's condition is interesting, the student's use of technical jargon appropriate, and the little humorous comment at the end, all provide a lot of information about the student: interest and experience in robotics, pragmatic (and cool) approach to problem-solving, computer and technology confident, tenacious and calm, confident in leadership, and a sense of humor. That's a very good start!

3   Sum up the theme of your essay in one thesis statement
Your thesis statement should appear as the last sentence in your opening paragraph to lead on to the rest of your supporting evidence in the following paragraphs. In relation to a leadership theme and the engineering student's opening comments above, some examples of strong thesis statements could be:

"All strong leaders are good communicators", or "Every great leader has overcome failure in his or her life."

4   Write three paragraphs of body text
The body text should support the argument outlined in your thesis statement. Following your introductory paragraph with three paragraphs of body text, and then a conclusion, allows you to follow the classic format for a five-paragraph essay.

- Each paragraph of the body text section should contain a different argument and evidence that support your thesis. The first body text paragraph should feature your strongest argument;
- Each paragraph of body text should be between three and five sentences long;
- Throughout your body text, write clear examples and anecdotes that enhance your arguments. For instance, if your thesis is, "Communication is the most important characteristic of leadership," give examples of how you or strong leaders throughout history have embodied this trait;
- Use information from your research to support claims and arguments.

Remember, the five-paragraph model is a standard format that may not apply to all prompts. Restructure your essay according to the exact requirements in the application.

5   Write a strong conclusion
Your final paragraph is your last chance to convince your reader of your arguments.

- Do not introduce any new evidence in your conclusion;
- Your conclusion should include a re-phrasing of your thesis statement and a brief summary of your supporting arguments;
- Finish your conclusion with a final thought on the subject.

6 Evaluate content and scope of your essay
Try to incorporate ways of showing other aspects of yourself that are relevant to your overall story. For example, if you were co-leader of your robotics team and started a Farsi language club in high school, try to find ways to indicate how you successfully juggled the two activities.

FINALIZE
1   Re-read your essay
Once your essay is written, step away for a few hours or, if you have time, a few days. When you read it again, **read it out aloud**. You will immediately hear awkward sentences and wording and get a sense of cohesion and clarity. Consider these points:

- Does your essay answer the question(s) posed clearly and comprehensively?
- Did you follow the format, style, or length requirements listed on the application?
- Are there any grammar or typing errors to be corrected? (Do not rely only on your spellcheck).

2   Ask for feedback from a parent, teacher, or friend
It is always helpful to have another person read your essay. The Essay Evaluation table in the Parent Pointer section following provides guidelines for editing.

COLLEGE APPLICATION WRITING: ESSAYS, PERSONAL STATEMENTS, AND SUPPLEMENTS

5.9 THE COLLEGE APPLICATIONS ESSAYS AND SUPPLEMENTS TRACKER

The template below is a sample Essay/Supplements Tracker, essentially a list of ALL the writing you must do for the colleges to which you are applying. All of this information is on the Common Application and other applications, but it is can be helpful to have a paper copy pinned to your wall so that you can see what needs to be done and your progress.

Once you see what needs to be done, you are in a better position to determine if there are opportunities to 'cut and paste' essays from one source to another, such as, for example, cutting down a 650 word Common App essay to a 550 words Coalition App essay or one of the 350 words essays of the required four on University of California application. Because the Common Application essay is the most common of the college applications writing, it is used here as the foundation piece. However, the principles applied to this piece of writing are relevant to all other forms of writing for college applications.

Sample Essays and Supplements Tracker					
Type	Max Word count	Prompt/question	Draft	Final
Common Application	650	Discuss an accomplishment, event, or realization that sparked a period of personal growth and a new understanding of yourself or others.		
College A	250	Please briefly elaborate on one of your extracurricular activities or work experiences.		
College B	250	Please briefly elaborate on one of your extracurricular activities or work experiences.		
College B	100	How will opportunities at College B support your interests, both in and out of the classroom?		
College B	100	Briefly discuss your reasons for pursuing the major you have selected.		
College B Honors 1	500	Why this college?		
College B Honors 2		Leadership essay		
College C	5-500	In what ways are you a good match for this college's distinctive educational and campus experience?		
College D	300	Please briefly elaborate on one of your extracurricular activities or work experiences.		
College D	250	Why are you interested in in this college?		
College E	250	Please briefly elaborate on one of your extracurricular activities or work experiences.		
College E	250	Why are you interested in this college?		
College E	250	Tell us why you are pursuing your selected major. If you are undecided on a major tell us about the academic areas of interest to you.		

Go the extra mile. It's never crowded.

— Unknown

5.10 PARENT POINTER – HOW TO HELP IN THE ESSAY WRITING STAGE

HELP YOUR TEEN FIND A TOPIC FOR THE ESSAY
Finding their story is often the hardest part of the essay for many students. Parents can be of great help at this stage and, if handled well, their input is often welcomed. Here are a few pointers to help you help your teen at this crucial first stage of the essay:

1. ACKNOWLEDGE outright to your teen that the essay is a complex piece of writing. They will be more disposed to listening to you and talking to you if they feel that you understand that;

2. AVOID putting forward an idea with the opening question, "Why don't you write about..... ?" No matter how many interesting scenarios you come up with, your teen may only see it as another demand and, consequently, another opportunity to 'fail' if they don't do the essay on your suggested subject;

3. THE POWER OF PHOTOGRAPHS - Looking at photos of their younger selves, significant people in their life, holiday experiences, award ceremonies, matches won, and goals scored can all help a teen contextualize their life and see that it has been full and interesting. At a time when virtually all teens are friend-centered, a reminder of family experiences, loving relatives, and fun activities can spark all sorts of memories, feelings, and - a story. You can help them think about the relationship between image and story by saying things like, "Uncle David was a great trumpeter – I wonder if you got your love of playing from him" or, "Grandma was such a great cook, wasn't she? Her lemon meringue pie was the best." Be genuine and share your experiences of those images, and allow time for your teen to think and, hopefully, come up with some ideas too.

4. ASK THEIR OPINIONS - Another tip to helping your teen find a story is to ask questions that enable him or her to think about their reactions to particular events rather than the events themselves. This means asking open-ended questions and then listening. Instead of asking what they thought about summer camp last year, ask who their favorite counselor was and why, or ask what their favorite activity was and why. As your teen talks, listen for 'cues' in their descriptions. For example, when your daughter talks about her favorite program counselor, Clare, she might tell you that it was Clare who encouraged her to go up on stage and sing in front of the whole group. This is your cue to ask her how it felt to be believed in by someone other than her parents, and how it felt being up on stage. Was she afraid? How did she overcome her fear? Was it difficult to find that first note? Try not to connect the experience to a story just yet, and just give her time to talk about the experience, which will lead her to thinking about the impact it had on her and if it is important enough to her to write about.

If you are lucky enough to have this kind of conversation with your teen, try to imagine you are speaking to a friend. You may want to 'tell' them what they must write about or what they should be thinking about a particular experience, but that would be unwise: the moment you do that, your teen may shut down the conversation and be loathe to discuss the subject with you again.

HELP WITH PROOF-READING AND EDITING
If your teen has asked you to review his or her essay, you should consider it a compliment and responsibility. It is also important that your teen see you take the time to read it. Try not to 'take it to the

office' or tell them that you'll 'do it later' without giving a specific time. Show them that you appreciate their trust in you and that you respect the task. Ways to help could be:

- *Tell your teen exactly when you will read the essay. Be mindful that, if they have written a draft, they are 'in the (college applications) zone' and will appreciate a timely response;*

- *At the time you specified for the task, indicate to your teen that you are going to be reading it and take it to a quiet space on your own;*

- *Read the paper out loud (alone) and make a note in the margin to parts that feel 'unnatural' to read;*

- *Read the essay again. For grammar editing, read by sliding a rule down the page, line-by-line. For full edit, make notes paragraph by paragraph. You will be looking at Content, Format, Tone, and Grammar. See the Essay Evaluation Notes below for suggestions of what to look for;*

- *When 'presenting' your comments to your teen, be mindful that they have worked hard and could be a little sensitive to criticism. Always start on a positive note, saying, for example, that you like the theme, the style of writing, or the story as a whole. Then, carefully, take them through your comments, perhaps using the Evaluation rubric on the following page for your comments.*

REVIEW EVERY APPLICATION
At the end of it all, and no matter what it takes or what arguments your teen may have, you – or another adult invested in your child's future - should REVIEW EVERY APPLICATION and ensure that:
- *Every question is answered;*
- *All information required is provided and correct;*
- *All parent information is complete and correct;*
- *The essays are perfectly written (see editing tips in the following table);*
- *All supplements, including relevant 'optional' essays, are complete and perfect.*

Essay Evaluation Notes	
Points to evaluate	**Comments/Notes**
Content Is it interesting? Is it too personal? What is the theme or main point? Are there too many/too few ideas? Has your teen shown progression or understanding of him/herself?	
Format Does the essay flow? Is each paragraph roughly the same length? Is the opening sentence 'catchy'? Why? Repetition of ideas, statements, words? Awkward language or sentence structure? Wording - slang, exaggerated (awesome, fantastic), thesaurus-driven (i.e. not natural to your teen)	
Tone Can you 'hear' your teen's voice in the essay? What qualities does your teen reveal through the narrative? Does your teen sound confident? Is there a satisfying conclusion? Does it relate to opening theme?	
Grammar Spelling Punctuation Sentence structure Are there any awkward phrases or terminology? Acronyms (should be written in full first mention with acronym in brackets. Acronym can be used thereafter)	

Life affords no greater responsibility, no greater privilege, than the raising of the next generation.

— C. Everett Koop

CHAPTER 6

SUBMISSIONS AND BEYOND

You're braver than you believe and stronger and smarter than you think.

- Winnie-the-Pooh

6.1 COLLEGE ADMISSIONS PLANS

Most colleges offer a variety of application submission options, which are:

REGULAR DECISION
Most colleges have a deadline for the submission of applications, generally from 15 December onward. In this admission plan, students are informed of the college's decision any time before early April and are required to respond to an acceptance notification by 1 May.

ROLLING ADMISSIONS
In this plan, College admissions officers review applications in the order they are received, and applicants are notified of decisions generally within six to eight weeks. As colleges with rolling admissions send out their acceptances early in the academic year, it is to the student's benefit to apply as soon as possible. Many state universities use this plan. Even though a college with a Rolling Admissions policy accepts students early, however, students do not need to notify the college of their decision until 1 May.

EARLY DECISION (ED)
Some colleges have an early decision plan, whereby the student is bound into a contractual agreement with the college to attend that college should their application be accepted. Early Decision students generally apply by early November and the admissions committee will review the student's application earlier than those applying by the regular deadline. Typically, the committee will inform the student of its decision in December or January. Through this plan, the student is committed to attend that college and must withdraw applications to other colleges. A student may submit only one Early Decision application.

Some colleges offer an Early Decision plan with a later application deadline, usually in December, January, or February. Some colleges offer an additional Early Decision date, known as Early Decision 2 (ED II). The student is informed of the college's decision within four to six weeks and, as with Early Decision, it is binding.

Advantages of Early Decision:

- If you are absolutely certain that you want to attend a particular college, your application process will be concluded if you are admitted;
- If you are a recruited athlete, applying ED helps to cement your commitment to a coach;
- If you are applying for financial aid, you may benefit from access to a full aid budget in November as opposed to waiting for Regular Decision when the admissions process can sometimes become "need aware;"
- An Early Decision application, coupled with a special 'hook', such as athletics, can be a real advantage in the process.

Disadvantages of Early Decision:

- The Early Decision pool of applicants typically consists of very strong candidates, making the competition potentially harder than in the regular pool;
- Financial aid rewards are, at this point, only estimates, so if the size or nature of your financial package is important, you may not want to turn your back on all other options;
- If you are deferred, it can feel like rejection at a time when you need to be strong and positive for completing applications to other colleges;

- When you are deferred, you automatically go into the regular applicant pool and your application may not look as impressive as those belonging to applicants who have had several extra weeks working on their application;
- There is also the possibility that you will be denied early, which presents another set of potential emotional turmoil at the time when you really do need to be 'on your game.'

EARLY ACTION (EA)
Early Action is an application submitted early but without the obligation to attend that college.
Some colleges offer options of two Early Action dates.

Advantages of Early Action:

- Attractive option if you have narrowed down your college choices;
- If you are a strong applicant, your application will be reviewed in a smaller group of applicants;
- If you are admitted under EA, you may decide to enroll at that college and conclude your application process or apply to one or two others with the 'safety net' of a college place.

Disadvantages of Early Action:

- You need to be a strong applicant to be competitive in this early pool.

SINGLE CHOICE EARLY ACTION
Just as it says, this plan means that you can apply early to only one college and you are not obliged to attend if accepted. Some colleges have other restrictions and some change their early action plans. It is advisable to always consult the college's website to ensure that you abide by their policies.

6.2   SUBMISSIONS SCHEDULE AND RESPONSE TRACKER

When you have finalized your college choices, you will then decide on when you are going to submit the applications. Unless you are applying Early Decision, and if rules allow, it is a good idea to apply Early Action to as many of your colleges as possible. To do this, you must be happy with your SAT or ACT scores so that the colleges see you at your best. Below is an example of a staggered submissions schedule. In this case, you can see that three Early Action responses came in before the end of the year:

Sample Submissions Schedule					
Early Action 1-Nov Submit 15 Oct	Response by	Regular Decision 30-Nov Submit by 22 Nov	Response by	Regular Decision 1-15 Jan 2017 Submit by 15 Dec	Response by
College A	15-Dec	College E	Mid Mar	College I	End Mar
College B	15-Dec	College F		College J	
College C	20-Dec	College G	End Mar		
College D	15-Jan	College H			

As the results come in, it's a good idea to create a table with the key benefits of each of the colleges that have offered you admission and your personal notes as reminders of what you consider memorable about each college. A Response Tracker, such as the example below, is particularly useful when it comes to decision time:

Response Tracker				
College	Scholarship/ Funds	Honors/other program	Notes/Special considerations
College A	No	Honors program	Great music program
College B	5,000 p.a.	No	Nice vibe/ laid back
College C	No	No	Boston, great vibe
College D	14,000 p.a.	Honors college	Lots of friends attending

6.3 RESPONSES: ACCEPTANCES, DEFERRALS, AND WAIT LISTS

ACCEPTANCES

Congratulations! You are going to college! If you applied to private colleges, you may also find yourself in the fortunate position of having been offered money to entice you to attend. If that is the case, congratulate yourself and bask in the glory of knowing that a college appreciates you and wants you. You should keep track of your responses and, specifically, the incentives they may offer.

DEFERRALS

If you were deferred from your top choice college, don't despair – it may not be over. You can write a powerful letter or email to your admissions representative about your first semester and noteworthy news of your accomplishments since you submitted your application last fall. Some suggestions on how to update the college include:

- Tell them of your ongoing interest in the college. Mention any new contacts with the college, department, alumni, or current students. If you have visited the college since your application, and particularly if you spoke to any professors or sat in on a class, mention that too;

- Highlight your academic accomplishments from first semester. Include a piece of work of which you are particularly proud and on which you did well. Give a brief explanation of why this piece of work was important to you. If it is a group project-based piece, indicate your role in the group, especially if you were the leader;

- Describe any new activities or accomplishments within existing activities. For example, if you have a part-time job, indicate if you have taken on added responsibilities, such as handling of money, or managing people;

- Connect your accomplishments to programs and activities at the college that you would like to pursue. For example, if you worked in a shop or restaurant and were responsible for reconciling accounts at the end of the day, you could mention that you enjoyed this aspect of the job and could see yourself in a treasurer role within the many clubs, organizations, or societies within the college;

- Remind them of your ongoing passion for the college and of something key about you from your initial application. If you founded your high school's robotics team or started a club or society, remind them. If you rowed for the past four years or spent the last two summers working in refugee camps in Greece, tell them;

- Conclude your letter by telling the college how grateful you are that they are still considering you and that this college continues to be your first choice.

WAIT LISTS

Being put on a wait list offers you a ray of hope, but you must be realistic. Colleges can wait list from 100 to 2,000 students. However, if you really want the college, you can try the following strategies:

- Take action and let the admissions department know that the college is your first choice and you REALLY want to attend. Ask what you can to do increase your chances;

- Send extra letters of recommendation, especially ones that pertain to your field of study and/or highlight how you can contribute to the college's academic community;

- If you have raised your grades, tell them. Also, let them know about any new honors or awards you have received or new involvement in community service and activities;

- Let them know if you don't need financial help or if you have received scholarships;

- Ask for an interview (or another one);

- Reconsider the colleges that accepted you. Remember, you are their FIRST choice.

- If you *really* love the college, you can ask about ask about 'multi-entry admissions' for enrollment in spring, winter, or summer, or, if the colleges offers it, 'multi-location admission' for enrollment at other campuses in the U.S. and/or overseas. Many colleges are beginning to offer these kinds of options to keep their seats full.

- The National Association of College Admission counselors (NACAC) website, www.nacacnet.org posts colleges that have openings for their freshmen class AFTER the May 1 deadline. Check out the 'Space Availability' section and survey state-by-state lists of colleges to which you can still apply.

REJECTIONS

If you received a rejection from your favorite college, you may try to appeal the decision and you must act quickly: It shows your interest and the college may have a few spots available for appeals. If you are persistent, it might work. You should:

- Check the college website for information on the appeals process. This information is often difficult to find on a college's website, but a good place to start is the Counselor link. If you are unsure about appealing the decision, talk to your counselor for advice;

- Write a letter and provide new information and briefly state your reason for appealing. Include your semester grades, a letter of recommendation from a teacher, counselor, coach, employer, or youth director. Two letters should be adequate and include all the information in one envelope;

- Some colleges have an April 15 or earlier deadline for an appeal. You should get a reply around May 1. Since May 1 is the official deadline to let a college know of your intent to register, you need to accept another college's offer. If your appeal is successful, you will be allowed to withdraw from one college and accept the new offer. Be aware that you will most likely lose your deposit and possibly priority for housing;

- Update information from your original application and include grades and test scores. Remember to also provide relevant documentation;

- Inform the college of any award you won since you submitted your application;

- Divulge personal circumstances that may be pertinent to a college's reconsideration, such as personal hardship or family issues.

Send your letter of appeal, official sealed and signed transcript, and other supporting documents in one envelope. Your Counseling Office will give you the transcript in a sealed envelope with the registrar's signature on the outside of the envelope. Do not open it! Buy a large envelope and take it to the Post Office for the correct postage. You can email in advance, but it is likely that your appeal will not be considered with email correspondence alone.

"The only person you are destined to become is the person you decide to be."

- Ralph Waldo Emerson

6.4 PARENT POINTER – HELP IN THE DECISION-MAKING PROCESS

The wait is finally over and all the responses are in. Your teen must now make the decision of which college to attend. You can help in the decision-making process in several ways:

- *Be a sounding board as your teen discusses all the options with you;*

- *Discuss with your teen the factors that he or she feels are most important considerations for their college experience;*

- *Suggest building a template to consolidate all the information, to include your child's important factors, details of the offers, and notes about each college that your teen found compelling during visits or research. See the template below for suggestions on what to think about.*

DECISION TIME - COLLEGE COMPARISON CHECKLIST

TOP PRIORITY	COLLEGE A	COLLEGE B	COLLEGE C	COLLEGE D
1. Strong English/writing program	Yes - renowned for it	Kind of - but not as strong as I'd like	Creative writing is a big draw card here	Very good - journalism focus
2. Study Abroad program	Good program in South Africa	Yes, in biz program	Limited choices	Yes, in biz program
3. Urban campus	No - but nice campus	Yes - in L.A.	Suburban	Yes - in Chicago
4. Business program	Yes - renowned for it	Good economics	Pretty good	Good International Biz program
5. Greek life	Yes	Yes	No	No
6. Scholarship	12,000 p.a.	No	15,000 p.a.	8,000 p.a.
7. Honors Program	Yes	No, but test-in option	No	Yes

The student who completed this template had seven most important factors to consider, all listed in order of importance (to her) in the left-hand column. She narrowed down her seven offers to her four favorite (Colleges A, B, C, and D) which she was having difficulty choosing between. With her parents, she worked through each college's offerings against her most important criteria. After a lot of soul-searching, this student decided to commit to college A. She decided that, although an urban campus was something she thought she wanted, she realized that, for her, the many other opportunities that college A offered outweighed that one factor.

A goal should scare you a little, and excite you a lot.

- Joe Vitale

CHAPTER 7

ADVICE FOR INTERNATIONAL STUDENTS

"Don't let your dreams be dreams"
- Jack Johnson

7.1 STUDYING IN THE UNITED STATES

In conversations or articles regarding higher education in the United States, the term 'college' is used interchangeably with the term 'university' and even 'school.' There are formal differences between universities and colleges (explained in Chapter 3), such as the types of programs offered, facilities, and populations, but in general usage, 'college' is the most common term in everyday language and refers to both universities AND colleges. For example, the college applications process refers to the applications process for colleges and universities.

Recent figures show that approximately 30% of all international students studying today are in the United States. American universities are world-renowned for the quality of their teaching and research and for their versatile and flexible education system. The following information may be useful when considering studying in the United States:

Academic Excellence

The U.S. has one of the finest education systems in the world, with excellent programs across all disciplines. At the undergraduate level, there are outstanding programs available in conventional subjects, professional fields, and a variety of more eclectic disciplines. Qualifications awarded by U.S. universities are recognized globally for their excellence.

Diversity of Education Opportunities

The structure of higher education programs stress equal emphasis on teaching a strong theoretical base as on practical, employment-related skills. The variety of programs, the scope and depth of teaching within them, and the hands-on practical experience that many universities offer are outstanding.

Cutting-Edge Technology

U.S. universities are world leaders in technology and scientific techniques and they are committed to providing the same resources to students, with particular emphasis on acquainting students with the latest developments, equipment, and ideas in the fields of science, engineering, and related fields. Graduates are equipped with the appropriate skills and knowledge of the most recent technology and are prepared for the challenges of the work in their fields.

Opportunity for Research, Teaching, and Training

Many smaller universities offer research opportunities at the undergraduate level, giving students the opportunity to engage with their subjects at a more advanced level than in other academic institutions around the world. The practical experience gained is extremely useful for future careers in teaching and research.

Flexibility

The U.S. higher education system offers many course choices within a program and the opportunity to specialize in several areas of study. The system is flexible enough for students to change majors if they wish. At the advanced stages of an undergraduate program a student can tailor the program to meet specific career aspirations.

Support Services for International Students

U.S. universities welcome international students and have support systems to help students adjust comfortably to life in the U.S. The international student office at a college offers services to help students transition to the new environment. Support is offered through the year from organizing orientation programs to assistance with academic writing and résumés.

Campus Life

U.S. universities offer a diverse choice of academic, cultural, and athletic activities that not only enrich the educational experience but also help students make new friends and become global citizens. Many colleges have clubs, societies, and organizations that are focused on languages, culture, and activities that can help international students feel 'at home.'

Global Education

A U.S. education enhances a student's potential in the international job market. The critical thinking skills, self-confidence, and cross-cultural skills that a student acquires from an American college education are all highly valued by employers worldwide.

Being allowed to study in the U.S. is a process; one that requires a lot of planning and focus. International students wishing to apply to universities in the U.S. will have to do many of the same things that domestic students do, all of which are detailed in the previous chapters, but international students must also complete several other conditions within various areas of the process, the most important of which include:

7.2　ADMISSIONS

Applying to college in the United States is a long and complicated process for American students; for international students, it can sometimes seem overwhelming. The three most important aspects to think about before you begin thinking about the college applications themselves are: admissions, funding, and visas.

Most universities in the U.S. require foreign applicants to take an English as a second language test, such as the Test of English as a Foreign Language (TOEFL) or the International English Language Testing System (IELTS). It is worth noting, however, that most colleges generally prefer TOEFL.

The applications process for international students follows along the same lines as for American applicants. For example, international students are generally required to take standardized tests, such as the Scholastic Aptitude Test (SAT) or ACT exams. These tests should ideally be completed in the August of the year before you want to start college. Application deadlines for international students are also generally the same as for American applicants, but it is always a good idea to check.

The Common Application (also referred to as the Common App) is the largest centralized processing hub for college applications. With a membership of over 800 colleges, it is likely that at least one of the colleges you wish to apply to will use the Common App. You will therefore need to complete this and provide required information, essays, and documentation. Details of completing the application are in Chapter 4 and guidelines on college applications essay writing are in Chapter 5. Depending on how many colleges you apply to, it is possible that you will have several pieces of writing to do, so it is advisable that you give yourself plenty of time to work on those.

Colleges have a variety of applications submissions deadlines, which are generally the same for American and international students. They are:

- Early Action and Early Decision deadlines are generally 10 months before the course starts: mid-October or early November. If you are accepted by an early decision, you are legally bound to attend that institution, so you should only apply for an early decision for one college that you are certain you would want to attend;

- Regular decision deadlines can vary, and exact dates should be noted for each college to which you apply. Some have end-of-year deadlines (i.e. eight months before you intend to start). Many have January deadlines (i.e. seven months before you intend to start) and some will have deadlines as late as March, or even later;

- Rolling admissions policy means that colleges evaluate applications as they are received versus waiting to evaluate all applications after a hard deadline. Colleges continue to evaluate applications until they've filled all the spaces for their incoming class. Unlike early action and early decision, rolling admission is not an option you choose, but is the way certain colleges run their admission process.

- Each application will almost always require:

    An application form (see types of applications in Chapter 4);
    An application fee for each college that ranges from $40 to $90;
    A personal essay and, often, supplementary writing;
    References;
    A transcript of academic achievements;
    Standardized test results (SAT, ACT, SAT Subject tests);
    Financial statements;
    Possibly Visa details.

7.3 FUNDING

American colleges offer two types of funding: <u>financial aid</u>, which is awarded on the basis of need, and <u>scholarships</u>, which are awarded for academic excellence. Much of this funding is reserved for domestic students and is very competitive for international students. Whilst it is not common for international students to secure funding for their first year of undergraduate study, however, it is common for them to secure it for the second year onwards. It should be noted that funding rarely covers the full cost of tuition and there may be obligations to funding awards, e.g., the student must work for the college as part of the funding agreement.

For merit-based scholarships, your high school grades and test results need to be significantly higher than average. Some college scholarships are designated for people with specific attributes, such as country of origin, ethnicity, faith, or gender, and some on academic interests, personal qualities, and talents.

Needs-based financial aid takes into account you and your family's ability to pay tuition fees.
Some colleges offer full needs-based scholarships that cover any cost of tuition that your family cannot demonstrably pay, and only consider financial needs after you have already been accepted, rather than as a detail of your application. Some of the largest and most well-known colleges adopt this policy, such as, the Massachusetts Institute of Technology, Harvard University, Princeton University, Yale University, Dartmouth College and Amherst College.

Financial aid applications often require a College Scholarship Service (CSS) Profile Form and/or other documents to assess your financial need. The actual requirements vary between colleges and it is therefore essential that you check with each of the colleges to which you are applying.

The Education USA financial aid search tool can help you to find suitable funding opportunities. It is important to note that international students applying for aid at American colleges are not eligible for federal aid, and as a result, find themselves in a much more competitive group for aid from the college's institutional resources. However, there are colleges that have financial aid specifically for international students. According to a US News report in October 2018, 451 colleges in the U.S. awarded aid to 50 or more international students and, of those, the top ten schools awarding the most aid to the most number of international students were:

Columbia University, NY	Amherst College, MA
Harvard University, MA	Wesleyan University, CT
Skidmore College, NY	Duke University, NC
Williams College, MA	Wellesley College, MA
Trinity College, CT	Vassar College, NY

For more information of financial aid to international students, it is advisable to research websites and/or call a college's international office.

7.4 VISAS

With changes in immigration policies, visa requirements for students may also change and it is therefore advisable that you check online at https://travel.state.gov/content/travel/en/us-visas/study/student-visa.html for the latest information on visas for international students in the U.S. Currently, the U.S. visa requirements are divided into three categories for students:

- F1 for academic studies;
- J1 for practical training not available in your home country;
- M1 for vocational studies.

If you are applying for an academic degree or English language course, you will need the F1 visa, which is the most common visa for international students. Things to consider are:

- Under the terms of this visa, you are obliged to return to your home country within 60 days of completing your degree;

- You will have to pay a visa application fee and must have been accepted at a U.S. college when you make the application;

- The visa is only valid to study at that specific college. It is possible to transfer to another college, but there are more forms to complete and further steps that you will need to take;

- You will have a visa interview and will be required to prove that you have sufficient funds to support your studies and that you have strong ties to your home country through family connections, assets, bank accounts or some other means;

- The visa permits you to work in the U.S. during your studies.

If you want to stay in the U.S. for up to 12 months after your studies, the Optional Practical Training (OPT) Program allows international students on F1 visas to do so if they gain employment in their field of study.

Graduates of science, technology, engineering, or Mathematics can extend their OPT by a further 17 months and stay for just over two years to work in these areas. You must apply for OPT before completing your studies.

The J1 visa applies to specialist programs and projects that provide training that you could not otherwise get in your home country, e.g., a business trainee program, an internship program, and a physician program. Some of these programs involve college study, but many are only for practical training. For the most part, you will not apply for this visa to study in the U.S. unless there is some agreement with an intended employer or between your government and a project in the U.S.

The M1 visa is for vocational studies. Students cannot work during the visa period, although they can undertake practical training or part-time work relevant to their studies. This visa is only available to students at an accredited trade or technical school.

7.5   Application Tips for International Students

Standardized Tests: For students who are used to a different curriculum and test style, the SAT and ACT can be daunting. Familiarizing yourself with structure, content, and style of the tests by taking practice tests will help you feel more comfortable with them. The SAT and ACT are equal in the eyes of U.S. colleges and you only need to choose one to take and submit.

If you are taking the SAT, the Khan Academy provides useful tutoring and tips. Sometimes some colleges will accept a student's own country's exams instead of a standardized test and many colleges are now becoming test-optional or have flexible test policies. Make sure that you are aware of the exact requirements for each of the colleges to which you are applying.

The Common Application (the 'Common App'): Getting through the Common App is a large part of the application process and many students find it intimidating. Once you get into the Common Application website (https://www.commonapp.org) and create a student account, however, you will see that it has a user-friendly interface. You should be aware that some of the questions may not apply to you, and it is advisable that you read all instructions carefully.

Apply to a lot of colleges, so you have options: Many international students focus only on the prestigious colleges, all of which are very difficult to get into. You should be aware that there are many excellent colleges you may not have heard of that acceptance rates of over 50% and offer financial packages. It is therefore worthwhile applying broadly to a variety of colleges.

Research scholarships and financial aid: College in the U.S. is expensive. If you are depending on potential scholarships to fund part of your costs, you must research extensively. It is essential that you examine and apply to all available scholarship opportunities and complete all the necessary paperwork within the deadlines.

Take the TOEFL (The Test of English as a Foreign Language): Generally, American colleges require international students to provide evidence of having taken and passed the TOEFL. Many international students take the IELTS (International English Language Testing System) and this is acceptable in UK and Australian universities, but TOEFL is the test that American universities generally prefer. If you take the IELTS, and a U.S. college is interested in you, it could require you to do another evaluation during orientation or to take English classes along with your regular courses, no matter how good your scores are. In this respect then, it is better to do TOEFL in the first place.

Grades matter within context of your study: Colleges require grades from 9th grade to 12th grade (years 9 – 12) and use a student's Grade Point Average (GPA) to evaluate their academic abilities. Many countries do not follow the GPA system and international students cannot submit such data. College admissions offices are aware that high schools around the world are different and will evaluate your grades on merit of the system within which they were achieved.

The essay is an important component of the application: You might be a really good writer but the college application essay is not just about grammar and good spelling. Indeed, it may be a different style of writing than many international students are used to. When writing your essay, it is advisable to have a teacher or counselor familiar with the American college system proofread it for you. Before attempting it though, you are advised to read as many sample essays as possible and work on different prompts to establish the right one for you. For guidelines on writing the essays and supplements, refer to Chapter 5.

If you are a minority student, let the colleges know: U.S. colleges are passionate about diversity and inclusion and most want to open their doors to talented minority students. The best way to use this to your advantage is your personal essay, in which you are able to describe, for example, how being in a minority has made you the person you are. If you have triumphed over challenges, college admissions officers will recognize that as a significant attribute in a student.

Select colleges based on your major: Many U.S. students apply to college with no idea of what they plan to study or 'major' in. The process of college allows for the fact that students can explore different areas and decide one or two years down the line what they actually want to study. International students generally do not have that luxury, particularly if they are applying to highly ranked colleges. If you choose colleges based on a defined area of study (a major), you will have many options. It is worth remembering that some lesser-known colleges might be the best for your major. Even though they may not be colleges you have heard of, they may be the colleges that will give you the kind of learning experience that surpasses your expectations.

Attend a College Fair: International students who attend National College Fairs have the opportunity to meet representatives from colleges from around the U.S. The following tips will help you to make the most of your college fair experience:

- Register beforehand - If you pre-register, you can skip the long registration line at the fair;
- Get to the venue early - College fairs can get very busy, so it is wise to get there early. When you arrive, pick up a map and plan which colleges you want to visit first. Leave time to browse around the desks of other universities as you may find something that interests you;
- Have a plan - Make a list of the colleges that you definitely want to visit;
- Get connected - Make sure you get on the mailing lists of all the colleges in which you are interested. Generally, all college representatives use the bar code system to take a student's details, but just in case there is any technical error, and you don't want to be writing out your address and email at every booth, make a few address cards (with area of academic interest if you have one) to hand out if necessary.

Have a mentor: College guidance counselors are very busy people in American high schools. They help students with their college choices, ensure that they are on track with high school classes, and write recommendations for every student who applies to college. Most international high schools do not have such an official and so it is vital that you have someone you can trust to help you navigate the administrative issues.

Plenty of time to decide on a major: Unlike applying to universities in other countries where you are expected to declare an area of study, this is not necessarily the case in the U.S., where you can wait one or even two years before making a decision about specializing. In the U.S., students are expected to take about five subjects per semester and then declare a major (the main subject that you will graduate in) at the end of sophomore year (2nd year). Most colleges offer a whole host of different subjects and students will often take subjects that have little or nothing to do with their final major. The opportunity to continue to study a variety of subjects is one of the most attractive aspects of college in the U.S. You should be aware of two particular exceptions to this:

- If you are interested in specific areas, such as engineering, medicine, and nursing, you may need to apply directly to the particular department within the college;

- Many colleges want to know your area of interest (rather than specific subject) and will often ask this question on the application. Showing your orientation towards the arts or sciences, for example, gives the college admissions officers enough information to help them build a balanced freshman (1st year) class, with equal representation of students in various disciplines.

Research colleges with a high percentage of International Students: The best way to get updated information on the percentage of international students at each college is to look at a college website or search for the information in list form. Recent figures from the U.S. News 2019 show U.S. national universities and liberal arts colleges with an international student percentage of 10% or more, as shown in the following tables:

National Universities with international student populations of 10% and above						
College	State	% of international students	College	State	% of international students
Florida Institute of Technology	FL	32	University of Pennsylvania	PA	13
The New School	NY	32	University of Southern California	CA	13
University of Rochester	NY	24	Arizona State University--Tempe	AZ	12
Boston University	MA	22	Drexel University	PA	12
Carnegie Mellon University	PA	22	Lindenwood University	MO	12
Suffolk University	MA	22	Michigan State University	MI	12
Brandeis University	MA	21	Morgan State University	MD	12
Illinois Institute of Technology	IL	21	Pennsylvania State U--University Park	PA	12
University of California--San Diego	CA	20	Princeton University	NJ	12
New York University	NY	19	Rice University	TX	12
Northeastern University	MA	19	Robert Morris University	PA	12
University of Tulsa	OK	19	University of California--Berkeley	CA	12
Andrews University	MI	18	University of California--Los Angeles	CA	12
University of California--Irvine	CA	17	University of Massachusetts--Boston	MA	12
University of San Francisco	CA	17	University of Oregon	OT	12
Emory University	GA	16	Brown University	RI	11
Purdue University- West Lafayette	IN	16	George Washington University	DC	11
University at Buffalo-SUNY*	NY	16	Harvard University	MA	11
University of California--Davis	CA	16	Pepperdine University	CA	11
University of Illinois Urbana-Champaign	IL	16	Worcester Polytechnic Institute	MA	11
University of Miami	FL	15	Yale University	CT	11
University of Washington	WA	15	Cornell University	NY	10
Clark University	MA	14	Duke University	NC	10
Miami University--Oxford	OH	14	Indiana University--Bloomington	IN	10
Rensselaer Polytechnic Institute	NY	14	Johns Hopkins University	MD	10
Stony Brook University--SUNY	NY	14	Massachusetts Institute of Technology	MA	10
Cardinal Stritch University	WI	14	Pace University	NY	10
Case Western Reserve University	OH	13	Tufts University	MA	10
Georgetown University	DC	13	University of California--Santa Barbara	CA	10
Syracuse University	NY	13	Wake Forest University	NC	10
University of Chicago	IL	13	*SUNY - State University of New York		

Liberal Arts Colleges with an international student population of 10% and above

College Name	State	% of international students	College Name	State	% of international students
Soka University of America	CA	43	Lawrence University	WI	12
Mount Holyoke College	MA	27	Trinity College	CT	12
St. John's College	NM	26	Wesleyan University	CT	12
Bryn Mawr College	PA	23	Pomona College	CA	11
College of the Atlantic	ME	22	Skidmore College	NY	11
Earlham College	IN	22	U. Minnesota-Morris	MN	11
St John's College	MD	22	Bard College	NY	10
Grinnell College	IA	20	Carleton Colege	MN	10
Principa College	IL	18	Colby College	ME	10
Bennington College	VT	17	Denison University	OH	10
Claremont McKenna College	CA	17	DePauw University	IN	10
Knox College	IL	17	Drew University	NJ	10
Franklin & Marshall	PA	16	Harvey Mudd College	CA	10
Bard College at Simon's Rock	MA	15	Houghton College	NY	10
Beloit College	WI	15	Lafayette College	PA	10
Macalester College	MN	15	Middlebury College	VT	10
Wesleyan College	GA	15	Oberlin College	OH	10
Smith College	MA	14	St. Olaf College	MN	10
College of Wooster	OH	13	Wheaton College	MA	10
Dickinson College	PA	13			
Sarah Lawrence College	NY	13			
Swarthmore College	PA	13			
Wellesley College	MA	13			

Potential for Culture Shock: The first week of college at the vast majority of U.S. colleges is a chance for students to get to know each other, sign up to clubs, societies and fraternities, and attend parties and events held by your college. There will be a whirlwind of activity as you try to remember names, find your way around campus, and keep up your energy levels to stay engaged and involved. There can be the potential for feeling disorientated and out of your depth. Try not to worry – it will settle down and you will find 'your people' and your way around the campus within a short time.

Textbooks are expensive: This is worth mentioning because it is such a shock to many international students that textbooks in the U.S. are extremely expensive. Fortunately, bookshops, social media groups, E-bay, and Amazon provide services to trade, share or pass on second-hand textbooks, so it is worth checking out all these avenues before buying brand new books.

U.S. college life is relaxed, but grading is not: Many international students are confused by the disparity they find between the relatively relaxed atmosphere of lectures (addressing professors by their first names, for example) and the apparent carefree vibe of the student community, and the extremely tough grading systems of the colleges themselves. Often, making even the slightest error with citations or essay structure can severely reduce a grade or render it a fail. It is important to check and double-check all the work that you submit.

Look beyond the Ivy League: The Ivy League colleges are renowned for their quality and prestige. The colleges that make up the Ivy League - Brown, Columbia, Cornell, Dartmouth, Harvard, Princeton, University of Pennsylvania, and Yale - are incredibly competitive, most with admission rates well below 10%. When a variety of factors are taken into account (such as legacy students and athletes, for example) that admissions percentage is reduced. It is therefore wise to look beyond the Ivy League colleges to the many other great colleges in the U.S. Depending on the course or experience you want, you will find many colleges that will suit you and that will want you in their student body. Whatever strategy you decide upon when applying to universities in the U.S., it is highly advisable to spread your options and apply to colleges with a variety of admissions rates. You may well find a college to which you are better suited – and one that may even offer you money to attend too.

Flexible study: U.S. colleges are highly flexible when it comes to changing courses or classes. You can change your major as many times as you like if you feel it doesn't suit you. There is generally also flexibility in changing colleges and transferring credits from one institution to another.

College sports are a big part of the experience: In the U.S., college sports are a huge part of the college experience. Students are expected to support their college teams, go to the games, and wear the logo t-shirt. Whether you are a sports fan or not, supporting the college team is an essential part of college life. For international students, it is an easy and enjoyable way to get involved in the college culture and community.

I am not the same for having seen the Moon shine on the other side of the world

- Mary Ann Radmacher

A Final Word

This book is designed to help you through one of the most exciting and challenging periods of your academic life. Wherever you go to college, remember with pride that this was a time in your life when the whole world was open to you and you took charge of your own destiny.

I wish you everything you wish for yourselves.

Susan McGarr, Ph.D.

May the Force Be With You.

- Star Wars

COLLEGE ADMISSIONS GLOSSARY

A

Academic adviser: A member of a school's faculty who provides advice and guidance to students on academic matters, such as course selections.

Academic year: Annual period during which a student attends and receives formal instruction at a college or university, typically from August or September to May or June. The academic year may be divided into semesters, trimesters, quarters, or other calendars.

Accredited: Official recognition that a college or university meets the standards of a regional or national association. Although international students are not required to attend an accredited college or university in the United States, employers, other schools, and governments worldwide often only recognize degrees from accredited schools.

ACT (American College Test): A standardized college entrance exam administered by the American College Testing Program. Four separate, multiple-choice tests measure knowledge of English, math, reading, and science, and one optional writing test measures essay planning and writing skills. Most students take the ACT during their junior or senior year of high school, and most colleges and universities accept scores from either the ACT or SAT. Some schools may recommend, but not require, international students to take the ACT or SAT. (See the U.S. News college test prep guide for more information.)

Affidavit of Support: An official document proving adequate funding from an individual or organization to cover an international student's educational and living expenses while enrolled at a U.S. college or university.

AP (Advanced Placement program): A program offered by the College Board, a U.S.-based nonprofit educational organization, that allows students to take college-level courses while in high school. Students can then take standardized AP exams; those with qualifying scores can earn credit at certain colleges and universities.

Articulation Agreement: Formal arrangements between two or more colleges and universities that specify how courses, a general education plan, and/or major requirements transfer from one institution of higher education to another. Articulation agreements are crucial for transfer students who need to understand how their credits will translate to other institutions.

Arts Supplement is a supplement to the Common Application that allows students to submit visual, audio and video media displaying their artistic talents. For students applying to art programs, an Arts supplement or portfolio is required by most programs and plays an important role in the admissions decisions.

Assistantship: A financial aid award granted to a graduate student to help pay for tuition that is offered in return for certain services, such as serving as a teaching assistant or research assistant.

Associate's degree: An undergraduate degree awarded by a college or university upon successful completion of a program of study, usually requiring two years of full-time study. An associate's is typically awarded by community colleges; it may be a career or technical degree, or it may be a transfer degree, allowing students to transfer those credits to a four-year bachelor's degree-granting school.

Audit: To take a class to gain knowledge about a subject, but without receiving credit toward a degree.

B

Bachelor's: An undergraduate degree awarded by a college or university upon successful completion of a program of study, typically requiring at least four years (or the equivalent) of full-time study. Common degree types include Bachelor of Arts (B.A. or A.B.), which refers to the liberal arts, and Bachelor of Science (B.S.). A bachelor's is required before starting graduate studies.

C

Campus: The grounds and buildings where a college or university is located.

Campus Interview: An optional component of the admission process where the student schedules a visit with an admissions officer.

Campus Tour: A visit university campus that include opportunities to take a guided tour, observe campus culture, talk to current students, sit in on a class, and visit the surrounding community.

COLLEGE ADMISSIONS GLOSSARY

Class Rank: A measure used to show how a student's academic performance compares to that of their peers within the same high school class.

CLEP: The College Level Examination Program is a group of standardized tests created and administered by the College Board. These tests assess college-level knowledge in over 30 subjects and provide a mechanism for earning college credits without taking college courses.

Coalition Application: A college application accepted by more than 140 colleges and university. The application platform also offers a set of free online college planning tools that help students learn about and prepare for college.

Coed: Open to both men and women (often used to describe a school that admits both sexes and a dormitory that houses both genders).

College: A postsecondary institution that typically provides only an undergraduate education, but in some cases, also graduate degrees. "College" is often used interchangeably with "university" and "school." Separately, "college" can refer to an academic division of a university, such as College of Business. (See U.S. News's rankings of Best Colleges.)

College Essay: A common component of the admission process that allows students to showcase their individuality.

College Fair: An event for students and parents at which college admissions representatives from colleges around the country set up information booths to promote their schools, and to answer questions and provide information.

Commencement: A graduation ceremony where students officially receive their degrees, typically held in May or June at the end of the academic year, though some colleges and universities also hold August and December ceremonies.

Common Application (often referred to as 'Common App'): A standard application form that is accepted by more than 800 member colleges and universities for admissions. Students can complete the form online or in print and submit copies to any of the participating colleges, rather than filling out individual forms for each school. International students will typically need to submit additional application materials unique to each college.

Community college: A public, two-year postsecondary institution that offers the associate degree. Also known as a "junior college." Community colleges typically provide a transfer program, allowing students to transfer to a four-year school to complete their bachelor's degree, and a career program, which provides students with a vocational degree.

Conditional admission: An acceptance to a college or university that is dependent on the student first completing coursework or meeting specific criteria before enrollment. For an international student, this can include a requirement to attain a certain level of English-language proficiency if the student's TOEFL score doesn't meet the minimum required.

Core requirements: Mandatory courses that students are required to complete to earn a degree.

Course: A regularly scheduled class on a particular subject. Each college or university offers degree programs that consist of a specific number of required and elective courses.

Course load: The number of courses or credits a student takes during a specific term.

Credits: Units that a school uses to indicate that a student has completed and assed courses that are required for a degree. Each school defines the total number and types of credits necessary for degree completion, with every course being assigned a value in terms of "credits," "credit hours," or "units."

Curriculum: A program of study made up of a set of courses offered by a school.

D

Dean: The head of a division of a college or university.

Deferral / Deferred admission: A school's act of postponing a student's application for early decision or early action, so that it will be considered along with the rest of the regular applicant group. A "deferral" can also refer to a student's act of postponing enrollment for one year, if the school agrees.

Deferred Enrollment: A decision made by the student to postpone their admission to college, sometimes used to take a 'gap year.'

Degree: A diploma or title awarded to students by a college or university after successful completion of a program of study.

Demonstrated interest: Various ways in which a student shows their interest in attending a specific institution prior to the official application process. Measures of demonstrated interest vary from college to college, but can include taking a campus tour, contacting the admissions office, and/or registering for an overnight program on campus.

Department: A division of a school, made up of faculty and support staff that gives instruction in a particular field of study, such as the history department.

Discipline: An area of academic study.

Dissertation: An in-depth, formal writing requirement on an original topic of research that is typically submitted in the final stages before earning a doctorate (Ph.D.).

Doctorate (Ph.D.): The highest academic degree awarded by a university upon successful completion of an advanced program of study, typically requiring at least three years of graduate study beyond the master's degree (which may have been earned at a different university). Ph.D.

candidates must demonstrate their mastery of a subject through oral and written exams and original, scholarly research presented in a dissertation.

Dormitories (dorms): Student housing provided by a college or university, also known as "residence halls," which typically includes rooms, bathrooms, common areas, and possibly a kitchen or cafeteria.

Double major: A program of study that allows a student to complete the course requirements for two majors at the same time.

Drop: To withdraw from a course. A college or university typically has a period of time at the beginning of a term during which students can add or drop courses.

Dual degree: Program of study that allows a student to receive two degrees from the same college or university.

E

Early Action (EA): Students apply by an earlier deadline to receive a decision in advance of the college's Regular Decision notification date. Students will not be asked to accept the college's offer of admission or to submit a deposit prior to May 1st.

Early Decision (ED): Students commit to a first-choice college and, if admitted, agree to enroll and withdraw their other college applications. Colleges may offer Early Decision I (ED 1) or Early Decision 2 (ED 2) with different deadlines. This is the only application plan where students are required to accept a college's offer of admission and submit a deposit prior to May 1st.

Electives: Courses that students can choose to take for credit toward a degree, but are not required.

English as a Second Language (ESL): A course or program of study used to teach English to non-native English speakers.

Enroll: To register or enter a school or course as a participant.

Exempt: Not required to do something that other students may be required to do. For example, a school may require all students to take a freshman English course, but some students may be exempt based on their high scores on a college entrance exam or their previous coursework.

Extracurricular activities: Optional activities, such as sports, that students can participate in outside of academic classes.

F

Faculty: A school's teaching and administrative staff who is responsible for designing programs of study.

Federal Application for Federal Student Aid (FAFSA): Required application for anyone filing for federal financial aid, including all federal loans.

Fees: An amount of money charged by colleges and universities, in addition to their tuition, to cover costs of services such as libraries and computer technology.

Fellowship: An amount of money awarded by a college or university, usually to graduate students and generally based on academic achievement.

Financial Aid: Monetary assistance applied toward postsecondary education, which can consist of gift-aid, work-study, or loans.

First-Generation: College applicants who are the first in their families to apply ad attend a postsecondary institution.

Fraternity: A student organization, typically for men, formed for social, academic, community service, or professional purposes. A fraternity is part of a college or university's Greek system. Some fraternities, such as those with an academic or community service focus, may be coed.

Freshman: A student in the first year of high school or college / university.

Full-time student: A student who is enrolled at a college or university and is taking at least the minimum number of credits required by the school for a full course load.

G

Gap Year: A student's decision to postpone their acceptance to college, usually during the year between senior year of high school and freshman year of college.

GMAT (Graduate Management Admission Test): A standardized graduate business school entrance exam administered by the nonprofit Graduate Management Admission Council, which measures verbal, quantitative, and analytical writing skills. Some business schools accept either the GMAT or GRE. In June 2012, the GMAT will incorporate an integrated reasoning section designed to assess how applicants analyze different types of information at once. (See the U.S. News business school test prep guide for more information.)

Grade: A score or mark indicating a student's academic performance on an exam, paper, or in a course. A "grade" can also refer to which year a student is in while at elementary, middle, or high school, but that usage typically does not apply at the college or university level.

COLLEGE ADMISSIONS GLOSSARY

Grade Point Average (GPA): A component on high school transcripts that averages a student's grades, typically on a 4.0 scale. Some schools give more weight to grades earned through higher-level coursework and the scale is then 5.0.

Graduate school: The division of a college or university, or an independent postsecondary institution, which administers graduate studies and awards master's degrees, doctorates, or graduate certificates. (See U.S. News's rankings of Best Graduate Schools.)

Graduate student / graduate studies: A student who already holds an undergraduate degree and is pursuing advanced studies at a graduate school, leading to a master's, doctorate, or graduate certificate. A "graduate" can also refer to any student who has successfully completed a program of study and earned a degree.

Grant: A type of financial aid that consists of an amount of free money given to a student, often by the federal or a state government, a company, a school, or a charity. A grant does not have to be repaid. "Grant" is often used interchangeably with "scholarship."

GRE (Graduate Record Examination): A standardized graduate school entrance exam administered by the nonprofit Educational Testing Service (ETS), which measures verbal, quantitative, and analytical writing skills. The exam is generally required by graduate schools, which use it to assess applicants of master's and Ph.D. programs. Some business schools accept either the GMAT or GRE; law schools generally require the LSAT; and medical schools typically require the MCAT. Effective August 2011, the GRE will incorporate key changes in the content, length, and style of the exam. (See the U.S. News GRE guide for more information.)

Greek life/Greek system: A college or university's collection of fraternities and sororities on campus, whose names originate from letters in the ancient Greek alphabet.

H

High school: A secondary school that offers grades 9 to 12.

Historically Black Colleges and Universities (HBCUs): Postsecondary institutions established prior to the Civil Rights Act of 1964 for the purposes of educating African-American students.

Honors classes/courses: Generally refer to exclusive, higher-level classes that proceed at a faster pace and cover more material than regular classes.

Humanities: Academic courses focused on human life and ideas, including history, philosophy, foreign languages, religion, art, music, and literature.

I

Independent study: An academic course that allows students to earn credit for work done outside of the regular classroom setting. The reading or research assignment is usually designed by the students themselves or with the help of a faculty member, who monitors the progress.

Institute: An organization created for a specific purpose, usually for research, that may be located on a college or university's campus.

Internal Revenue Service (IRS): The U.S. government agency that collects income taxes. International students who work on or off campus or receive taxable scholarships must pay taxes. A college or university's international student adviser can provide further information, including on relevant tax treaties between the United States and specific countries that may allow certain benefits.

International student adviser: A school official who assists international students, scholars, and faculty with matters including orientation, visas, income taxes, insurance, and academic and government rules, among other areas.

Internship: An experience that allows students to work in a professional environment to gain training and skills. Internships may be paid or unpaid and can be of varying lengths during or after the academic year.

Ivy League: An association of eight private universities located in the northeastern United States, originally formed as an athletic conference. Today, the term is associated with universities that are considered highly competitive and prestigious. The Ivy League consists of the highly ranked Brown University, Columbia University, Cornell University, Dartmouth College, Harvard University, Princeton University, University of Pennsylvania, and Yale University.

J

Junior: A student in the third year of high school or college / university.

Junior college: A two-year postsecondary institution that offers the associate degree. (See "community college.")

L

Latin Honors: three levels, each with its own minimum GPA requirement: Summa Cum Laude (With Highest Honor) – 3.90 GPA, Magna Cum Laude (With Great Honor) – 3.70 GPA, Cum Laude (With Honor) – 3.50 GPA.

Legacy: A student applicant with familial ties to the college or university to which they are applying.

Letter of recommendation: A letter written by a student's teacher, counselor, coach, or mentor that assesses his or her qualifications and skills. Colleges, universities, and graduate schools generally require recommendation letters as part of the application process.

Liberal arts: Academic studies of subjects in the humanities, social sciences, and the sciences, with a focus on general knowledge, in contrast to a professional or technical emphasis. "Liberal arts" is often used interchangeably with "liberal arts and sciences" or "arts and sciences."

Liberal arts college: A postsecondary institution that emphasizes an undergraduate education in liberal arts. Most liberal arts colleges have small student bodies, do not offer graduate studies, and focus on faculty teaching rather than research. (See U.S. News's rankings of Best Liberal Arts Colleges.)

Loan: A type of financial aid that consists of an amount of money that is given to someone for a period of time, with an agreement that it will be repaid later. International students are generally not eligible for U.S. federal government loans and will typically require an American cosigner to apply for a private bank loan.

LSAT (Law School Admission Test): A standardized law school entrance exam administered by the nonprofit Law School Admission Council, which measures reading comprehension, analytical reasoning, and logical reasoning skills. There is also a writing section; although it is not scored, it is sent to each law school to which a student applies. (See the U.S. News LSAT test prep guide for more information.)

M

Major: The academic subject area that a student chooses to focus on during his or her undergraduate studies. Students typically must officially choose their major by the end of their sophomore year, allowing them to take a number of courses in the chosen area during their junior and senior years.

Master's: A graduate degree awarded by a college or university upon successful completion of an advanced program of study, typically requiring one or two years of full-time study beyond the bachelor's degree. Common degree types include Master of Arts (M.A.), which refers to the liberal arts; Master of Science (M.S.); and Master of Business Administration (M.B.A.).

Matriculate: To enroll in a program of study at a college or university, with the intention of earning a degree.

M.B.A.: A master of business administration degree.

MCAT (Medical College Admission Test): A standardized U.S. medical school entrance exam administered by the nonprofit Association of American Medical Colleges, which measures verbal reasoning and writing skills and physical and biological sciences knowledge. The MCAT will likely undergo significant changes in 2015, with new areas added, such as genetics, cell and molecular biology, psychology, and sociology.

Merit aid / merit scholarships: A type of financial aid awarded by a college or university to students who have demonstrated special academic ability or talents, regardless of their financial need. Most merit aid has specific requirements if students want to continue to receive it, such as maintaining a certain GPA.

Midterm exam: An exam given after half of the academic term has passed and that covers all material studied in a particular course until that point. Not all courses have midterm exams.

Minor: An academic subject area that a student chooses to have a secondary focus on during their undergraduate studies. Unlike a major, a minor is typically not required, but it allows a student to take a few additional courses in a subject different from his or her major.

N

NCAA: National Collegiate Athletic Association (NCAA) – championship sports categorized into division levels. To be part of NCAA, colleges must offer at least four sports and have at least one in fall, winter, and spring seasons.

Need-based financial aid: Financial aid that is awarded to students due to their financial inability to pay the full cost of attending a specific college or university, rather than specifically because of their grades or other merit.

Need-blind admissions: A college or university's policy of accepting or declining applications without considering an applicant's financial circumstances. This policy does not necessarily mean that these schools will offer enough financial aid to meet a student's full need. Only a handful of U.S. colleges or universities offer need-blind admissions to international students.

Net price calculator: An online tool that allows students and families to calculate a personalized estimate of the cost of a specific college or university, after taking into account any scholarships or need-based financial aid that an applicant would receive. By Oct. 29, 2011, each higher education institution in the United States is required by law to post a net price calculator on its respective website.

Nonmatriculated: Enrolled in a college or university's courses, but not in a program of study leading to a degree.

Nonresident: A student who does not meet a state's residence requirements. A college or university may have different tuition costs and admissions policies for residents versus nonresidents. In most cases, international students are considered nonresidents. A "nonresident alien" is a person who is not a U.S. citizen and is in the country on a temporary basis.

Notarized: Certified as authentic by a public official, lawyer, or bank. Colleges and universities often require international students to submit notarized documents, such as the Affidavit of Support or high school transcripts.

COLLEGE ADMISSIONS GLOSSARY

O

Open admissions: A college or university's policy of accepting all students who have completed high school, regardless of their grades or test scores, until all spaces are filled. Most community colleges have an open admissions policy, including for international students.

Orientation: A college or university's official process of welcoming new, accepted students to campus and providing them with information and policies before classes begin, usually in a half-day or full-day event. Many colleges and graduate schools offer a separate orientation just for international students to cover topics such as how to follow immigration and visa regulations, set up a U.S. bank account, and handle culture shock.

P

Part-time student: A student who is enrolled at a college or university but is not taking the minimum number of credits required for a full course load.

Pass-fail: A grading system in which students receive either a "pass" or "fail" grade, rather than a specific score or letter grade. Certain college or university courses can be taken pass-fail, but these typically don't include ones taken to fulfill major or minor requirements.

Ph.D.: A doctor of philosophy degree. (See "doctorate.")

Placement Test: A test given to students before they enroll in college, and usually after they are accepted, to align their educational needs with the appropriate coursework.

Plagiarism: The use of another person's words or ideas as your own, without acknowledging that person. Schools have different policies and punishments for students caught plagiarizing, which tends to occur with research papers and other written assignments.

Post Doctorate: Academic studies or research for those who have completed a doctorate. A "postdoc" can refer both to a person who is pursuing a post doctorate and to the post doctorate itself.

Prerequisite: A required course that must be completed before a student is allowed to enroll in a more advanced one.

Priority date: The date by which an application must be received in order to be given full consideration. This can apply to admissions, financial aid, and on-campus housing. After the priority date passes, applications may be considered on a case-by-case or first-come-first-served basis.

Private College (also referred to as Private school or Private University): An academic institution financed primarily by tuition and endowments.

Probation: A status or period of time in which students with very low GPAs, or whose academic work is unsatisfactory according to the school, must improve their performance. If they are unable to do so, they may be dismissed from the school. Students may also face "disciplinary probation" for nonacademic reasons, such as behavioral problems in the dorms.

Professional school: A higher education institution for students who have already received their undergraduate degree to gain training in specific professions, such as law, medicine, and pharmacy.

Provost: The senior academic officer of a college or university who typically oversees all academic policies and curriculum-related matters.

PSAT: The Preliminary SAT, a standardized practice test cosponsored by the nonprofit College Board and the National Merit Scholarship Corp., which measures reading, writing, and math skills, giving students experience with the SAT. Students usually take the PSAT in their junior year of high school, and U.S. citizens and permanent residents can submit their scores to qualify for National Merit scholarships. (See the U.S. News college test prep guide for more information.)

Public college (also referred to as Public school or Public University): A postsecondary institution financed by tuition, endowments, and state or local taxes. Tuition for in-state students is reduced and programs and policies are state-regulated, operated by publicly elected or appointed officials.

Q

Quarters: Periods of study that divide the academic year into four equal segments of approximately 12 weeks each, typically including the summer.

R

Registrar: The college or university official who is responsible for registering students and keeping their academic records, such as transcripts.

Registration: The process in which students choose and enroll in courses to be taken during the academic year or in summer sessions.

Regular decision: An admissions process used by colleges and universities that typically requires applicants to submit their materials by January 1; an admissions decision is generally received by April 1, and if admitted, students usually have until May 1 to respond to the offer. The majority of applicants are evaluated during regular decision, rather than early action and early decision.

Resident assistant (RA): A student leader who works in campus dormitories and supervises issues and activities related to dorm life. RAs often receive free housing in the dorm in return for their services.

Restrictive Early Action (REA): Students apply to an institution of preference and receive a decision earlier than the regular decision date. They may be restricted from applying ED, EA, or REA to other institutions. If offered enrolment, students have until May 1st to confirm.

Retention Rate: The percentage of first-year students who continue at that college or university for a second year of studies.

Rolling Admission: Students apply at any time after a college begins accepting applications until a final closing date, which may be as late as the state of the term for which they are applying. Students are notified of a decision as their applications are completed and reviewed.

Room and board: Housing and meals. "Room and board" is typically one of the costs that colleges and universities will list in their annual estimated cost of attendance, in addition to tuition, fees, and textbooks and supplies. If students choose to live in dormitories, they may be required to buy into a meal plan to use on-campus dining facilities.

ROTC: Reserve Officers' Training Corps. U.S. armed forces offer ROTC programs that prepare candidates for commissions in the Air Force, Army, and Navy (including the Marine Corps). ROTC programs may take two or four years to complete.

S

SAT: A standardized college entrance exam administered by the Educational Testing Service (ETS) on behalf of the nonprofit College Board, which measures reading, writing, and math skills. Most students take the SAT during their junior or senior year of high school, and most colleges and universities accept scores from either the SAT or ACT. The SAT has changed names several times: previously the Scholastic Aptitude Test, the Scholastic Assessment Test, the SAT Reasoning Test, and now simply the SAT.

SAT Subject Tests: Standardized tests in English, history, languages, math, and science to demonstrate their knowledge in specific academic areas. Some schools may recommend, but not require, international students to take the SAT or ACT.

Scholarship: A type of financial aid that consists of an amount of free money given to a student by a school, individual, organization, company, charity, or federal or state government. "Scholarship" is often used interchangeably with "grant." (See the U.S. News scholarship guide for more information.)

School: Any educational institution, including those that provide elementary, secondary, and postsecondary education. In the latter case, "school" is often used interchangeably with "college" and "university."

Selectivity: Institutional statistic that compares the number of students who apply to those who are accepted.

Semesters: Periods of study that divide the academic year into two equal segments of approximately 15 to 18 weeks each. Some schools also offer a shorter summer semester, beyond the traditional academic year.

Seminar: A course offered to a small group of students who are typically more advanced and who meet with a professor to discuss specialized topics.

Senior: A student in the fourth year of high school or college/university.

SEVIS (Student and Exchange Visitor Information System): A computerized U.S. government database used to track international students and scholars in the United States. Once a college or university accepts an international student, it is required to mail the student a Form I-20, which is a paper record of the student's information in SEVIS. A student must pay a SEVIS fee and use the payment receipt and I-20 to apply for a visa.

Signature Project: a self-organized initiative addressing a need in the community, (re)inventing a product or service, or partnering with an uncommon organization working to achieve a goal. This extra-curricular project is intended for self-disciplined, high-achieving students who are inherently creative and want to challenge themselves.

Social Security number: A nine-digit number issued by the U.S. government to people who are authorized to work in the United States and collect certain government benefits. Many colleges and universities use the Social Security number as the student identification number. International students who are in the United States and are authorized to work, either on or off campus, must apply for and obtain a Social Security number, which is then used to report their wages to the government.

Sophomore: A student in the second year of high school or college/university.

Sorority: A student organization for women formed for social, academic, community service, or professional purposes. A sorority is part of a college or university's Greek system.

Standardized Tests: A national college admission exam of which the SAT and ACT are the most popular versions in US college admissions. Other Standardized Tests include the SAT Subject tests, taken at a student's discretion, in subject areas: English, Math, Sciences, History, and Languages. Most educational institutions use the SAT or ACT as one component for college admission consideration. SAT Subject tests are not widely required, except for home-schooled students.

Supplements (Supplementary Writing): Many colleges include their own school-specific essays, known as writing supplements. Admissions officers use these to: get to know the student better and gauge a student's demonstrated interest in the school and/or program.

Summer Melt

A trend describing students who apply and are accepted into college, but ultimately do not attend.

COLLEGE ADMISSIONS GLOSSARY

T

Teaching assistant (TA): A graduate student who assists a professor with teaching an undergraduate course, usually within his or her field, as part of an assistantship.

Tenure: A status offered to high-level faculty members at a college or university that allows them to stay permanently in their positions, after demonstrating a strong record of teaching and published research.

Term: Periods of study, which can include semesters, quarters, trimesters, or summer sessions.

Thesis: A formal piece of writing on a specific subject, which may be required to earn a bachelor's or master's degree.

TOEFL (Test of English as a Foreign Language): A standardized exam administered by the nonprofit Educational Testing Service (ETS), which measures English-language proficiency in reading, listening, speaking, and writing. Many U.S. colleges and universities require non-native English speakers to take the TOEFL and submit their scores as part of the admissions process.

Transcript: A student's academic history, usually curated by a high school counseling department, and submitted as a major component of the student's college application.

Transfer credit: Credit granted toward a degree on the basis of studies completed at another college or university. For instance, students who transfer from a community college to a four-year college may earn some transfer credit.

Tribal Colleges: Unique American institutions that offer opportunities for Native Americans to pursue higher education within their own cultural and regional contexts. Generally located on or near Indian reservations, tribal colleges and universities (also referred to as tribally controlled colleges) aim to preserve and communicate traditional native culture, provide higher education and career or technical opportunities to tribal members, enhance economic opportunities within the reservation community, and promote tribal self-determination.

Trimesters: Periods of study that divide the academic year into three equal segments of approximately 10 to 12 weeks each.

Tuition: An amount of money charged by a school per term, per course, or per credit, in exchange for instruction and training. Tuition generally does not include the cost of textbooks, room and board, and other fees.

U

Undergraduate student / undergraduate studies: A student enrolled in a two-year or four-year study program at a college or university after graduation from high school, leading to an associate or bachelor's degree.

University: A postsecondary institution that typically offers both undergraduate and graduate degree programs. "University" is often used interchangeably with "college" and "school."

V

Visa: An official mark or stamp in a passport that allows someone to enter a country for a particular amount of time. Common visa types for international students and scholars in the United States include the F-1 (student visa) and J-1 (exchange visitor visa). To apply for a U.S. visa, student applicants must first receive a Form I-20 from the college or university they plan to attend, which is created by the U.S. government's SEVIS database.

W

Wait list: A list of qualified applicants to a school who may be offered admission if there is space available after all admitted students have made their decisions. Being on a wait list does not guarantee eventual admission, so some students may choose not to remain on the list, particularly if the school is not their first choice.

Weighted grades: number or letter grades that are assigned a numerical advantage when calculating a grade point average (GPA). In some schools, primarily public high schools, weighted-grade systems give students a numerical advantage for grades earned in higher-level courses or more challenging learning experiences, such as honors courses, Advanced Placement (AP) courses, or International Baccalaureate courses. The terms quality points or honor points may also be used in reference to the additional weight given to weighted grades. In the case of students who have completed courses considered to be more challenging than regular courses, the general purpose of a weighted grade is to give these students a numerical advantage when determining relative academic performance and related honors such as honor roll or class rank.

Withdraw: To formally stop participating in a course or attending a university.

Work-study: A financial aid program funded by the U.S. federal government that allows undergraduate or graduate students to work part time on campus or with approved off-campus employers. To participate in work-study, students must complete the FAFSA. In general, international students are not eligible for work-study positions.

RESOURCES

Reference

College Admissions Data Sourcebook, Wintergreen Orchard House

The College Handbook, The College Board

The Book of Majors, The College Board

Scholarship Handbook, The College Board

College Costs & Financial Aid Handbook, The College Board

International Student Handbook, The College Board

Get it Together for College: A Planner to Help you Get Organized and Get In, The College Board

Paying for College, The Princeton Review

The Insider's Guide to College, Yale Daily News staff, St. Martin's Griffin

From Here to Freshman Year: Tips, Timetables, and To Dos that Get You into College, Kaplan Publishing, 2008

Books

Antonoff, Ph.D., Steven R., 2014, *College Match: A Blueprint for Choosing the Best School for You.*

Bedore, Dr. Deborah, 2015, *Getting In by Standing Out: The New Rules for Admission to America's Best Colleges*

Bleich, Lisa and Morgan James, 2014, *Surviving the College Application Process: Case Studies to help you find your unique success.*

Chisolm, Alison Cooper, Anna Ivey, Jossey-Bass 2013, *How to Prepare a Standout College Application.*

Dunbar, Dan, 2007, *What you Don't Know can keep you out of College*

Gelb, Alan, 2008, *Conquering the College Admissions Essay in 10 Steps.*

Blythe Grossberg, PsyD, 2011, *Applying to College for Students with ADD or LD: A Guide To Keep you (and your parents) Sane, Satisfied, and Organized Through the Admission Process.*

Eltgroth, Mike, 2015,*Think Where You're Going: The Must-Have Book for New Graduates Seeking Success in Life.*

Fiske, Edward B., *The Fiske Guide to Colleges*, 2018

Lewak, Risa, 2010, *Don't Stalk The Admissions Officer: How to Survive the College Admissions Process Without Losing Your Mind*

Jacobs, Lynn F, Jeremy S. Hyman Jeffrey Durso-Finley, Jonah T. Hyman, Jossey-Bass 2015, *The Secrets of Picking a College (and Getting In!)*

Lythcott-Haims, Julie, 2015, *How to Raise an Adult: Break Free of the Overparenting Trap and Prepare Your Kid for Success.*

Marcus, David L., 2009, *Acceptance: A Legendary Guidance Counselor Helps Seven Kids Find the Right Colleges – and Themselves.*

RESOURCES

McGinty, Sarah Myers, *The College Application Essay: Successful Strategies for a Winning Essay*, The College Board.

McMullin, Kevin d Robert Franek, The Princeton Review 2014, *If the U Fits: Expert Advice on Finding the Right College and Getting Accepted*.

Mitchell, Joyce Slayton, 2005, *Winning the Heart of the College Admissions Dean*.

Moyer, Mike, 2008, *How to Make Colleges Want You: Insider Secrets for Tipping the Admission Odds in your Favor*.

Pierce, Valerie with Cheryl Rilly, 2009, *Countdown to College: 21 'To Do' Lists for High School*.

Pope, Loren, 1995, *Looking Beyond the Ivy League: Finding the College That's Right for You*.

Pope, Loren, 2000, *Colleges That Change Lives*.

Quinn, M.D., Patricia O. and Theresa E Laurie Maitland, Ph.D., 2011, *On Your Own: A College Readiness Guide for Teens with ADHD/LD*.

Robinson, Janine, 2014, *Heavenly Essays: 50 Narrative College Application Essays That Worked*.

Rugg, Frederick, *Ruggs Recommendations on the Colleges*, 2019

Sawyer, Ethan, 2016, *College Essay Essential: A Step-by-Step Guide to Writing a Successful College Admissions Essay*

Schneider, Z.D. and N.G. Schneider, *Campus Visits & College Interviews*, The College Board

Springe, Sally P., Jon Reider, Marion R. Franck, Jossey-Bass, 2009, *Admission Matters: What Students and Parents Need to Know About Getting into College*.

Steinberg, Jacques, 2002, *The Gatekeepers*.

Tanabe, Gen and Kelly, 2009, *50 Successful Ivy League Application Essays*.

Wissner-Gross, Elizabeth, 2009, *Write Your College Essay in Less Than a Day*.

Websites
www.act.org
www.alumnifactor.com
www.bigfuture.collegeboard.com
www.blog.prepscholar.com
www.cambridgecoaching.com
www.cappex.com - College Scholarship information
www.coalitionforcollegeaccess.org
www.collegeboard.org - College Board – Information on AP, SAT and SAT Subject tests
www.collegeconfidential.com
www.collegeexpress.com
www.collegeinsight.com
www.collegeinsightpros.com
www.college-insight.org
www.collegesimply.com
www.collegepreparationinternational.com
www.college-prep-guide.com
www.collegesofdistinction.com
www.collegeraptor.com
www.commonapwwp.org
www.convinceandcovert.com
www.developgoodhabits.com
www.edglossary.org
www.educationulimited.com
www.fafsa.ed.gov - Federal Student Aid
www.getintocollege.com
www.getyourselfintocollege.com

www.greatvaluecolleges.net
www.grownandflown.com
www.hotcoursesabroad.com
www.huffpost.com
www.ibo.org - International Baccalaureate
www.internationalcollegecounselors.com
www.learn.org
www.mappingyourfuture.org
www.mycollegesuccessstory.com
www.mykidscollegechoice.com
www.nacacnet.org - National Association for College Admission
www.ncplanforcollege.com
www.nces.ed.gov - Federal Net Price Calculator
www.parenttoolkit.com
www.petersons.com
www.princetonreview.com
www.questions.blogs.nytimes.com
www.quora.com
www.scholarships.com
www.studentaid.ed.gov
www.theclassroom.com
www.theivycoach.com
www.thoughtco.com
www.topuniversities.com
www.urbandictionary.com
www.universityofcalifornia.com
www.universalcollegeapp.com
www.usnews.com
www.yougotintowhere.com

ABOUT THE AUTHOR

Susan McGarr, Ph.D. is an independent International Academic Consultant, Psychometrics practitioner, Teen Counselor, and Cognitive Behavioral Therapist. She provides academic and personal counseling to assess, enhance, and manage the aspirations and abilities of high school students who want to apply to college. She also advises parents on how and when to help their children with the many components of the process.

Dr. McGarr works with students throughout the United States and the world, advising on all aspects of the U.S. college applications process.

Website: www.susanmcgarrphd.com